UNSCRAMBLING AN EMPIRE
A CRITIQUE OF BRITISH COLONIAL POLICY
1956–1966

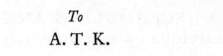

To
A. T. K.

UNSCRAMBLING AN EMPIRE

A Critique of British Colonial Policy 1956–1966

By

W. P. KIRKMAN

1966

CHATTO & WINDUS

LONDON

Published by
Chatto and Windus Ltd
42 William IV Street
London W.C.2

*

Clarke, Irwin and Co. Ltd
Toronto

Contents

Maps

Preface

FOR four years from the end of 1960 it was my good fortune to be deeply concerned, as a journalist, with colonial, Commonwealth and African affairs, which I covered both in London and during extensive travels in Africa. They were momentous years, which saw a rapid acceleration in the process of granting colonies their independence. In particular 1961 and 1962 were vintage years of colonial constitution-making. On occasion, for example, two constitutional conferences were taking place simultaneously.

Being in at the birth of new nations is an exciting experience even when the novelty of it has worn off. Personally, I am convinced that independence is both desirable and morally right. I believe that human beings should have the right to run their own affairs, to decide their own destinies, to make their own mistakes. For many years now, this has been the view of all the major British political parties, and colonial policy has not generally been a matter of political controversy. The journalist's responsibility of being accurate and objective was not therefore so hard to fulfil as it would have been had my own views been fundamentally out of tune with British policies, or if these policies had themselves been deeply controversial.

I make this point because this is a critical book, and I wish to emphasize that my criticisms are not of broad aims but of particular policies and particular methods adopted in striving at these aims.

Throughout nearly all the period covered by this book, a Conservative Government was in power. Inevitably, therefore, most of my criticisms are directed at Conservative Ministers and their policies. I hope it will be accepted that this is not because of political bias; as I have explained, colonial policy is not a party political issue. I have no reason to suppose that ministers of a Labour Government would have been noticeably more or less successful if the responsibility of the wind of change era had been theirs. I must also emphasize that there is no personal animus behind my criticisms. As a journalist I enjoyed excellent relations with ministers and other politicians. The relationship between press

7

and politician is always delicate. At its best it is intimate, but wary, and that is as it should be. It is certainly most important for a journalist to avoid commitment so that he can make his judgments uninfluenced by personal feelings. I have neither friends nor enemies among the politicians with whom I have had dealings, though we were, I hope I can truly say, on friendly terms. My criticisms are of policies, but as policies are evolved and carried out by people, criticisms cannot be impersonal.

In one respect I must qualify what I have just written about political detachment. When this book was nearly complete, the Southern Rhodesian unilateral declaration of independence was made. The situation demanded statesmanship by all this country's political leaders facing a situation widely misunderstood and of much greater gravity than many of the public recognized. The Conservative Party did not hesitate to support the Government at the beginning of the crisis. As the weeks went by, however, Conservative criticisms grew louder and voices from one section of the party began to be raised in support of the rebel Rhodesian régime. This happened when that régime was steadily increasing its repressive measures and was rejecting standards which in this country and in the civilized world generally are held to be sacrosanct. The Conservative Party leaders, though themselves continuing to support Government policy, failed to repudiate the Smith supporters among their following and by their failure they –unwillingly but avoidably– provided comfort to the Smith régime. This action, or inaction, of the Conservative leadership I found shocking, since this was not a question of policy, or of methods of carrying out a policy–where they quite rightly gave critical examination to what Mr. Wilson's Government did–but of deep and important principle.

To revert to my general theme, I am acutely aware of one great weakness of a commentator, however well informed. His is not the responsibility for making decisions or introducing policies. It may be that in some of the cases which I have discussed in this book, I would myself have adopted courses which I criticize, if I had known the same facts and been subjected to the same pressures as the men who actually had to decide. I can only say that I do not think many of the cases can be assessed in this way.

Working for *The Times* I counted a privilege. I could not have asked for a post more professionally satisfying than those which I held on that paper. I must emphasize that the views I have expressed in this book are my views and mine alone. I do not know whether *The Times* would share them. I certainly would not wish anyone to think that I wanted, even indirectly, to commit *The Times* to them.

W. P. KIRKMAN
Oxford,
May 1966

Acknowledgments

I AM grateful to the authors and publishers for permission to quote from the following works: J. G. Amamoo, *The New Ghana*, Pan Books, 1958; Ken Post, *The New State of West Africa*, Penguin Books, 1964; William Clark, *Occasional Paper No. 1*, Overseas Development Institute; Tom Mboya, *Freedom and After*, André Deutsch, 1963; John Hatch, *A History of Postwar Africa*, André Deutsch, 1965 and Praeger, New York, 1965; Sir Michael Blundell, *So Rough a Wind*, Weidenfeld & Nicolson, 1964; Dame Margery Perham, *African Outline*, Oxford University Press, 1966; Philip Mason, *Year of Decision: Rhodesia and Nyasaland 1960*, Oxford University Press, 1960; Sir Roy Welensky, *Welensky's 4000 Days*, Collins, 1964; Sir Charles Johnston, *The View from Steamer Point*, Collins, 1964; Dudley Barker, *Swaziland*, Corona Library, Her Majesty's Stationery Office, 1965; Robert Gardiner, Reith Lectures 1965, the B.B.C.; and Her Majesty's Stationery Office for numerous official publications, as detailed in the text.

I have quoted also from *The Times*, *The Financial Times*, *The Guardian* and *The Weekend Telegraph*.

I am grateful to Miss Caroline Parsons for so carefully and quickly typing my manuscript.

Introduction

WHEN India became independent in 1947, there were people in the India Office who expressed grave doubts whether as an independent country it would have enough trained people. India has had its troubles since independence but looking back most people would agree that the long heritage of the Indian Civil Service, the long tradition of impartial administration, had, by 1947, become an ingrained part of the Indian constitutional machine. Furthermore, with its vast size, its diversity of peoples, its highly developed culture and its resources, India was both politically and economically viable. Today, nearly twenty years after independence, it is still an under-developed country. It still needs large injections of foreign capital aid if it is to 'take off' economically. There is no question, however, that India makes sense as a nation. It meets the sort of criteria which in the 1940s and the 1950s were considered in Whitehall to be the essential prerequisites of independent nationhood.

When Nyasaland entered the final constitutional stage before independence, there were virtually no trained Nyasas to take even the key posts in the administration. By November 1963, Nyasaland's independence date was fixed for July 1964, its new name, Malawi, was chosen. Yet in that month, when I visited the country, I went to the Mpemba Institute of Public Administration near Blantyre to see students on a crash course in a training programme that was begun only a few months earlier.

By the mid 1960s, the old criteria had been dropped, and none had been put in their place. In 1964, no one raised an eyebrow at talk of independence for British Honduras, a country of about 100,000 inhabitants. In February 1965 The Gambia actually became independent. A 300-mile strip of land lying on either side of the Gambia river, flanked on three sides by Senegal, with an economy based, unsteadily and unprofitably, on peanuts, and with a population of only some 300,000, The Gambia on the morrow of independence could look forward to no brighter prospect than continuing dependence on the charity of the British Treasury and taxpayer. It came of age, in short, as a remittance state. It was not the first such state, but because it is particularly small, and because its geographical and economic position underline its problems

11

acutely to even the most superficial observer, independence for
The Gambia provoked a good deal of public discussion of the
standards and criteria for independence in the mid-1960s.

Of course, there are still people who can see no merit in the idea
of Africans ruling themselves, and who yearn nostalgically for the
'good old days' of colonial rule. Most of them admit that, even if
the maintenance of colonial rule were desirable, it would not be
practicable. However vaguely, most people recognize that the
phenomenon which Mr. Harold Macmillan called the wind of
change has been a force which could not be withstood, except
possibly, and for a limited time, by the exercise of blatant military
force. Few people, unfortunately, think very much about the
philosophy of independence. It is something that happens, with
due ceremonial and (in recent years) with almost boring frequency,
after a series of more or less stormy constitutional conferences
marked by walkouts, extremist manifestoes, compromises and,
ultimately, agreement reached often in the small hours of the night
to the accompaniment of mutual congratulation and hopeful leading articles in the press.

In the years when I have been closely following colonial and
African affairs, I have been basically in tune with the aims of
British policy in that sphere. The methods by which these aims
were sought, however, were not always quite so easy to accept.
Increasingly it has appeared that the challenge of history, the inexorable demands of the wind of change, have been met only
pragmatically, in a series of *ad hoc* decisions dreamed up to solve
immediate problems, with little thought given to long-term needs.
Colonial policy in the 1960s has been a series of tactical manœuvres
carried on in the absence of the necessary strategic framework. In
short, Britain, in the rush to divest herself (rightly and properly)
of empire has sometimes seemed to abandon policy altogether.

Of course, the right decisions have often been made. Sometimes
they have not. Sometimes, too frequently, expediency has been
permitted to outweigh principle. Probably the most glaring example
of this is the affair of the Federation of Rhodesia and Nyasaland,
created in 1953 and finally buried at the end of December 1963.
Whether the Federation should have been dissolved is a question
as controversial and as hotly argued as the earlier one: should it
ever have been formed? Whatever one's private views on this,
there is surely little room for disagreement with the opinion that

the British Government in the last years of the Federation's existence played a thoroughly unworthy role. Publicly stated policy until almost the very end was grossly at variance with what was in fact being done and planned. Sir Roy Welensky, in a conversation with me a few days before his term of office as Federal Prime Minister was to end with the disappearance from the map of the state over which he presided, mentioned the many criticisms of him which had appeared, over a long period, in *The Times*, which I then represented. He added that nevertheless *The Times* had always been absolutely straightforward with him and given him 'a fair crack of the whip', and he made the point that if the British Government had behaved equally openly with him, he would have had little to complain of.

He would, of course, still have complained, because what the British Government was doing and what Sir Roy Welensky wanted were diametrically opposed. He would still, quite probably, have pursued, in the Federal Government, policies that helped to make the demise of the Federation inevitable. But his point was valid; the end of Federation was inevitable, and was seen in Whitehall to be inevitable, but the pretence was kept up, in dealings with Sir Roy, that all was going to continue as before. One result of ambivalence over Central African affairs burst upon us in November 1965, when the minority government of Southern Rhodesia rebelled against the Crown, overthrew the constitution, declared the country independent and introduced much of the apparatus of a police state.

As the 1960s progressed and the pace of constitutional development increased, the British Government seemed to lose control over the situation, to be following a trend rather than initiating and pursuing a definite, properly conceived policy of disengagement. There were several signs of this. For one thing, there was the fundamental change in the accepted criteria for independence. For another, there was an increasing readiness to see the preparations for independence as a paper exercise of Lancaster House conferences, a challenge to chairmanship rather than a duty to find a constitutional framework genuinely acceptable to the people of the country concerned and relevant to their needs and conditions.

In the following chapters I shall examine some examples of recent colonial policy in detail and try to illustrate the truth of this generalization.

B

Chapter 1

Ghana - The First to Move

ON December 9, 1963, I attended in a sweltering court-room in Accra the last day's hearing in the trial of five men on treason charges. The men included two former ministers of the Ghana Government, Tawiah Adamafio and Ako Adjei, and a former executive secretary of the Convention People's Party, H. Cofie Crabbe. These three were acquitted by the three judges of the special court which had tried the case, in a long series of hearings.

The verdicts and sentences on the other two men who were found guilty came on a Monday. In Accra during the previous weekend, the case had been the main topic of conversation. Everyone who had followed the evidence as it unfolded over many weeks was convinced that, on the evidence, the two ex-ministers and the CPP official would be acquitted. One Ghanaian civil servant asked me what I thought the verdict would be. I said that I was not a lawyer and had anyway not followed the details of the case closely, but I added that, from what I had gathered, it ought to be an acquittal, and probably would be. He said that he had heard the same, and then remarked with a rather rueful smile: 'It would be a very good thing, wouldn't it.'

I had no reason to suppose that this man was anything but a loyal Ghanaian. Similarly, the people who packed the benches in the court-room on the Monday morning, sitting silently for two hours before the judges entered in the scarlet robes and white wigs which are still the visible inheritance of the British colonial régime, were certainly not dangerous revolutionaries, seeking to overthrow President Nkrumah's régime. Rather, they were men and women who sensed that high drama was about to be enacted, who guessed that the Ghanaian judiciary was about to strike one final blow in support of the rule of law, by returning a verdict in accordance with the evidence, but contrary to the wishes of the executive in the person of Dr. Nkrumah.

15

The spectators were not disappointed. Sir Arku Korsah, the Chief Justice and president of the special court, took five hours to read the judgment, calmly, and almost inaudibly. The two guilty verdicts came after the first and second hours. The three acquittals were announced only at the end of the long and careful review of the evidence relating to the three men concerned, and the announcement was greeted by gasps from the public seats.

That evening, I drove round Accra after cabling my report of the day's proceedings to *The Times*. The atmosphere was almost tangible. Police lined the approaches to Christiansborg Castle, where President Nkrumah was staying. I met a number of my friends, and every conversation I had convinced me that, although the expectation of high drama had that day been fulfilled, what we had experienced was only Act I. There was more to come.

Around midnight, I left, as previously arranged, for London. On the Wednesday, I went into *The Times* office, having been away in Africa for about six weeks. The Editor sent for me to hear at first hand my impressions of the situation in Ghana, at that time (as so often) going through a period of political and economic difficulty. I was asked: What is going to happen next? In general, this is a kind of question which one must answer cautiously, hedging one's reply with conditions, for predictions about the future of nations tend to be embarrassingly disproved. On this occasion, however, I did not hesitate but said at once: 'I shall not be surprised if the Chief Justice is sacked.' Within hours, news of his dismissal came across on Reuter's tapes.

My purpose in recounting this incident is not to demonstrate my skill as a prophet. Indeed, the whole point of it is that little skill was involved. From the way things were going in Ghana at the time of my visit, it was as clear as things can be before they actually happen that President Nkrumah would not tolerate any rival to his own supremacy. The apotheosis of the *Osagyefo*, the Redeemer-President, had already reached an advanced stage, and the exercise by a court of law of the prerogatives which it normally possesses under the British—and Ghanaian—constitutional systems was an intolerable infringement of the presidential power. Sir Arku Korsah, barrister of the Middle Temple for forty-four years, a judge since 1945 and Chief Justice since 1956, one of Ghana's most respected citizens, was arbitrarily dismissed in an action legally within the strict terms of the constitution but so far outside its spirit as to constitute a mortal blow to Ghana's international good name.

After this there were further developments to dismay Ghana's many friends, already saddened at the way in which President Nkrumah's policies were going. In February 1965, for example, another of Ghana's most respected sons, Dr. J. B. Danquah, died in jail, where he had been held without trial since early in 1964 (his second period of detention under President Nkrumah). Danquah was in a real sense the father of Ghanaian nationalism, and he was in fact responsible for inviting Dr. Nkrumah, then in London, to return home and take up in 1947 the position which so quickly brought him to the leadership of the nationalist movement, and to the van of the move to independence not only by the Gold Coast (as Ghana then was) but by Africa as a whole, following Ghana's lead.

Danquah was a lawyer of standing, and a scholar of some repute, but far more important, he was a man of deeply found principles. I called to see him in Accra during my 1963 visit, just a month before his final incarceration. He was under no illusions about his personal safety, but unlike most of the dissatisfied, who spoke, if at all, only in whispers and allusions, Dr. Danquah made no secret of his views. He knew perfectly well that his own days of freedom were numbered. President Nkrumah had already taken measures against him (and by implication against Sir Arku Korsah), the details of which Danquah told me himself. At the time, the story seemed no more than an example of presidential pettiness, but in the light of subsequent events, it assumes more sinister overtones, and is worth recounting (I believe for the first time).

In 1961 Sir Arku Korsah, in his capacity as chairman of the General Legal Council, asked Danquah to become editor of the Ghana Law Reports. Before he could take up the position, he was detained by the authorities for political reasons. By the time of his release, however, the interim editor had resigned to take another post, and once again Sir Arku Korsah asked Danquah if he would do the job. He agreed, and the appointment was confirmed by the General Legal Council, acting within its rights. Danquah wound up his private practice, and took up the editorial post on October 1, 1963.

Soon after this the General Legal Council received from Flagstaff House a letter from the Cabinet Secretary, expressing the displeasure of Osagyefo the President at Danquah's appointment 'having regard to the long history of Dr. Danquah's opposition to the Government and his [Dr. Nkrumah's] policies'. The letter added: 'Osagyefo has directed that if this is the way the General Legal Council is going to make use of the public funds at its disposal, then its subvention should be stopped.'

The General Legal Council considered the implications for the independence of the judiciary of this interference by the executive (in the person of the President) in a matter constitutionally the province of the council itself, but after careful thought it was decided that if they made an issue of principle of it, they would in all probability endanger the judicial position of those members of the council who held office by virtue of their judgeships. Accordingly, Dr. Danquah agreed to resign. In accepting his resignation, the council treated it as termination of the appointment without notice, and therefore paid him one month's salary in lieu of notice. They also wrote to Flagstaff House requesting that the President should receive Sir Arku Korsah and Sir Leslie M'Carthy (a member of the Council and a former judge) to negotiate the possibility of awarding to Dr. Danquah an *ex gratia* payment of four months' salary in the special circumstances. (He was short of money, having given up his practice.)

From Flagstaff House on November 16, 1963, the following reply came from the Cabinet Secretary to the secretary of the General Legal Council:

Dr. Danquah's letter of appointment provides for one month's notice for termination of the appointment, and although it does not specifically provide for cash payment in lieu of notice, it is noted that in accordance with normal practice you have properly paid him one month's salary in lieu of notice.

2. As Dr. Danquah's letter of appointment makes no reference to an *ex gratia* payment and since it is not the normal practice to make such a payment in addition to payment in lieu of notice, I regret to inform you that the Council's request cannot be approved.

This treatment of Dr. Danquah and the snub to the Chief Justice (who ranked next to the President, and had acted for him during his absences abroad) were signs of the sad state to which Ghana had been reduced by the end of 1963. The dismissal of the Chief Justice, and the gathering of still further powers into the

President's hands early in 1964 as a result of a plebiscite (conducted in a way that inspired little confidence in the validity of its result) on the constitution which finally made Ghana formally a one-party state, simply confirmed the trend. Understandably, when the three men acquitted by the 1963 court were tried again–and convicted–in 1965, no impartial observer could even imagine that they had received justice. (Their sentences of death were commuted by the President, following widespread international protests.)

This kind of development is splendid ammunition for those who maintain that Africans are incapable of governing themselves, and who feel that the granting of independence was a big mistake, a weak-kneed retreat before nationalist politicians–'self-appointed leaders', as the common description goes.

Are these people justified? Can the British Government of the day be blamed for putting power into the hands of President Nkrumah and his supporters? To my mind the answer must be an unequivocal 'No'. If you accept, as I do, that self-determination is a fundamental human right, it was entirely reasonable to transfer the political control of the Gold Coast to the party, and the leader, who commanded majority popular support.

Consider for a moment the history of the Gold Coast in the years immediately before independence. It is a story of skilful and effective political organization on the part of the Convention People's Party, launched in 1949 by Dr. Nkrumah. The background to the inauguration of the CPP was a growing rift in the leadership of the United Gold Coast Convention (UGCC) between the middle-class professional men (typified by Dr. Danquah) and the more dynamic 'mass' leaders, of whom Dr. Nkrumah became the supreme example. Danquah had founded the UGCC in the summer of 1947, and Kwame Nkrumah returned, at his invitation, from London to become its general secretary. With the formation of the CPP the position of the UGCC was undermined, and it eventually became submerged in another party (the Ghana Congress Party) in 1952.

The roles of the UGCC and the CPP in Ghana's independence movement are distinguished aptly by J. G. Amamoo, the Ghanaian author of *The New Ghana* (published by Pan Books in 1958). He wrote: 'If the honour of having awakened fervent national consciousness in the Gold Coast people belongs to the UGCC, to the

CPP must be given the credit of having kept alive that national consciousness.'

In practical terms, the difference between the two parties—and the thing which distinguished Dr. Nkrumah as the truly effective national leader—was their attitude to the common goal of independence. Danquah and his followers demanded 'self-government in the shortest possible time'. Dr. Nkrumah's demand was 'self-government now'. He announced that if he did not get it, he would launch a Gandhian campaign of civil disobedience and non-cooperation—'Positive Action' it was called.

Dr. Nkrumah, in short, had grasped the truth that the effective politician is usually not the man who argues intellectually to persuade an *élite*, but the man who can set before the people a clear choice, or a clear course of action, in terms which they can easily understand. This is not a specifically African phenomenon. You need only look at the election manifestoes of British parties, and see in how limited a way they deal with such complex topics as, for example, defence policy, to understand that it applies quite generally.

By the time of the foundation of the CPP a number of constitutional advances had already been made (quite substantial ones, given the much slower pace and much cooler political climate of the period by comparison with the 1950s and 1960s). Direct election in local government had been introduced in 1925. In 1946, under the Burns Constitution, a Legislative Council was formed on which African members were in a majority—the first time this had happened in British-ruled Africa. Following serious disturbances in 1948 the Watson Commission of Inquiry proposed various measures of constitutional reform and in 1949 the colonial government appointed a committee, composed entirely of Africans, under the chairmanship of Mr. Justice Coussey, which investigated the structure of the Gold Coast Government. The result was a new constitution under which elections were held in 1951.

In 1950 the country had come under a state of emergency after the introduction of the 'Positive Action' campaign. During the period of the 1951 elections Dr. Nkrumah was in jail. Nevertheless, the CPP won an almost total victory and Dr. Nkrumah himself was elected with a large majority. The Governor, the late Sir Charles Arden-Clarke, released him from prison, and invited him to form a government.

In the following year, 1952, he became Prime Minister, when that office was created by a constitutional amendment. In 1954, a new constitution was promulgated which provided for a cabinet consisting entirely of Africans, and direct elections to the legislature. In the Governor's hands remained only a few ultimate powers (responsibility for foreign affairs, defence and internal security).

Two years later, in May 1956, another general election took place, designed to pave the way finally for full independence. Once again, the CPP won hands down, obtaining more than two-thirds of the seats in the legislature. The Gold Coast Parliament requested independence under the name of Ghana, and the British Government agreed that independence should come in March 1957.

There is nothing remarkable in the stages of this constitutional progression. In recent years, we have seen colony after colony follow them. What is worthy of note in the case of Ghana, the first black African colony, British or other, to achieve its independence, is the time allowed for each stage. Even if we ignore earlier developments, and start in 1947 with the formation of the UGCC, we have a period of ten years, in which each new constitutional advance could be launched, tested and allowed to develop into the next step forward.

The 1951 elections demonstrated clearly that Dr. Nkrumah enjoyed wide popular support. After he had held office for five years, his position was put to the test again, in 1956, again with the same result. Only then was the Gold Coast released from Britain's colonial apron strings.

The political apprenticeship had been, by current standards, slow and steady. It is certainly possible to argue that it should have been slower, that more time should have been allowed for parliamentary traditions to grow up strong enough to replace the authoritarian traditions of colonial rule. Certainly, if you take the case of other countries in Africa which have followed Ghana's lead to independence, but in a far shorter span of time, you can make a good case for the desirability of delay. To such arguments I would counter that the independence movement has developed its own momentum, and that, however desirable, delay has often become impossible as a practical policy.

What is far more significant in the case of Ghana is the basic structure of the society on which the independence edifice was built. I have attended in Accra a dinner at which one of my fellow guests was a headmistress, a university graduate whose mother was a university graduate before her. That, in a continent where women generally are way behind men in their education, is a remarkable illustration of the relative sophistication of Ghanaian society. If you return to the incident with which I began this chapter, you will recall that Sir Arku Korsah, the then Chief Justice, was a barrister of over forty years' standing. If today you visit the principal secretary (i.e. professional head) of any of the Ghana government departments, you are likely to find an experienced official who would be quite capable of holding a senior position in, say, the British Civil Service. If you look at a list of Ghanaians who hold important positions outside their own country, you will find a number of able men, outstanding by any standards, such as Mr. Robert Gardiner, now running the United Nations Economic Commission for Africa, and formerly in charge of the U.N. Congo operation, and Mr. A. L. Adu, a former head of the Ghana Civil Service, who went to East Africa as Secretary-General of the East African Common Services Organization, then was appointed Regional Representative of the United Nations Technical Assistance Board in East Africa, and in October 1965 became one of the deputy secretaries-general of the Commonwealth Secretariat.

When the British Government decided to accept Ghanaian demands for independence in 1957, therefore, they were taking an historic step–setting Africa on the path which the Indian subcontinent had already trodden, with far longer preparation–but they were justified both by the political and the cultural background of the country. It was reasonable to assume that Ghanaians had the equipment necessary to run their own affairs. Incidentally, the Gold Coast possessed not only a strong and competent administration, but one of the strongest economies in Africa.

Under Dr. Nkrumah Ghana was ruled by an ideological group around the President and the role of the civil service was certainly nothing like the role prescribed for it by the British Government before independence, nor, indeed, its role in the early days of independence. Economically, Ghana got into a mess. Its reserves were eaten away, it was short of foreign exchange, consumer goods became hard to find, stringent fiscal measures became necessary, advice had to be sought from a mission sent by the International Monetary Fund.

Politically, the development of Ghana was a sad story. On independence, Ghana was in the van of pan-African politics. Dr. Nkrumah, having successfully won from the British the coveted prize of independence, was a leader respected and admired far outside his own country. Ghana was the model colony, the textbook example of the validity of British colonial methods. Then, Dr. Nkrumah's constant advocacy of a 'Union Government of Africa' as a means of achieving the unity to which all African leaders pay at least lip service, was supported by few of his colleagues. He was openly accused by the leaders of neighbouring states of planning and executing subversion against them. His treatment of political opponents drew upon him widespread protests, not just from outside Africa, but from his fellow Africans as well. When Danquah's death was reported Dr. Azikiwe, then President of Nigeria, delivered one of the most outspoken criticisms that anyone has made of Dr. Nkrumah. Dr. Nkrumah's party and government machines controlled press and radio, and the newspapers, in a country where the general standard of literacy is high by African standards, were filled with turgid and misleading propaganda. Outgoing press reports were subjected to censorship. Some newspaper correspondents were expelled or forbidden to enter the country. There were several attempts on the President's life. Senior police officers joined M.P.s and ex-ministers among the ranks of those detained without trial. A number of senior Ghanaians chose to work outside the country.

That the model of decolonization went badly wrong was agreed not just by the reactionaries who think that disaster must follow African rule as inevitably as night follows day. The progressives, the liberals, the supporters of the African nationalist cause, shared their dismay. Because things were so badly wrong, the tendency to argue that independence was all a mistake anyway was understandable. It has never, however, been a justifiable argument, since it misses the whole point of independence. The implications of a demand for or a grant of independence are clear. The fully sovereign state is, in a word, sovereign. It is fully and solely responsible for its own affairs, and it can arrange them as it likes. The result may be successful or unsuccessful. In either case, there can be no outside control. The colonial power grants independence, not independence if . . .

The classic instance is surely the Congo. It became independent in an ill-prepared rush in July 1960. Within days, the façade of administration was broken. The country erupted into chaos, and all the efforts of the United Nations and of individual countries could be no more than first aid. In strict fact, there was no Congolese Government. At times, the control of the central authorities has been so tenuous that it did not extend outside Leopoldville, the capital. And yet, because the Congo was formally an independent sovereign state, no one, legally, could act to alleviate its troubles without the agreement of the official government. The United Nations operation as a result was frequently hampered. But what is the alternative? The Congo is an extreme case, but if independence could be withdrawn when it was used in a way displeasing to the former colonial power (or anyone else), it would be meaningless.

This is a pretty obvious truth, but it is worth underlining simply because many people judge the performance and polity of the newly independent countries on the criteria of the west, rather than accept that their independence permits them to choose their own paths.

I had, of course, written the original draft of this chapter before the military action of February 1966 which ousted Dr. Nkrumah from power in Ghana, during his absence on a visit to Peking. The point I wished to make was that, however much one deplored what was happening in Ghana, it had to be recognized that it was happening under a properly constituted, effective government. The blame, in other words, must be laid at the door of the Ghana Government, or the Ghana people, or force of circumstances—but not of the British Government, unless it could be shewn that the preparations for independence were so inadequate, or so wrongly devised, that the successor régime could not possibly carry out the responsibilities devolving on it. This was, in my view, a valid argument for the Ghana of Dr. Nkrumah. The military coup strengthens it, since it illustrates that Ghana is not only juridically independent, but also that it is in fact mature enough to sort out its own troubles, to throw off its own dictator, and to do so with remarkable restraint and good sense.

Ghana, in short, was adequately prepared for independence. The Congo, manifestly, was not. I shall attempt to shew later that Britain also failed to prepare adequately some of its dependent territories.

Chapter 2

West African Patterns

GHANA entered independence with greater advantages than probably any other African country. Paradoxically, however, others offer better examples of well-grounded independence working out fairly well, because they did not suffer early political upheavals as serious as Ghana's. This is not to say that all has gone smoothly. At the time of the election in Nigeria, at the end of 1964, the first since the country became independent in 1960, political animosities and bitterness between the different peoples and regions of the Federation reached such a pitch that the continued existence of the Federation was seriously in doubt.

The causes of the crisis were complex, but essentially they arose from the wide disparity of background and outlook between the various parts of Nigeria, and in particular between the Northern Region and the three southern regions. To state the difference thus baldly is inaccurate, in that it ignores the complications of political alignment (different at the centre and in the regions), and the importance of personalities, but as an outline of the root cause of political strife this formula is valid. Because the North has a larger population than the southern regions put together (according to a census which itself was the cause of bitter controversy), the Northern People's Congress, the party of the North, won a majority in the election. Voting had in any case been boycotted by the National Convention of Nigerian Citizens (NCNC). This party, led by the Premier of the East, Dr. Michael Okpara, had in the previous government been the federal partner of the NPC, though throughout 1964 their differences had been more apparent than their agreements. Constitutionally the position was clear. Having won a majority, the NPC were entitled to form the government. Sir Abubakar Tafawa Balewa, the Prime Minister, waited for the summons from President Azikiwe.

The President comes from the East, and was formerly leader of the NCNC. Further, he is a man of strong personality, and as one

25

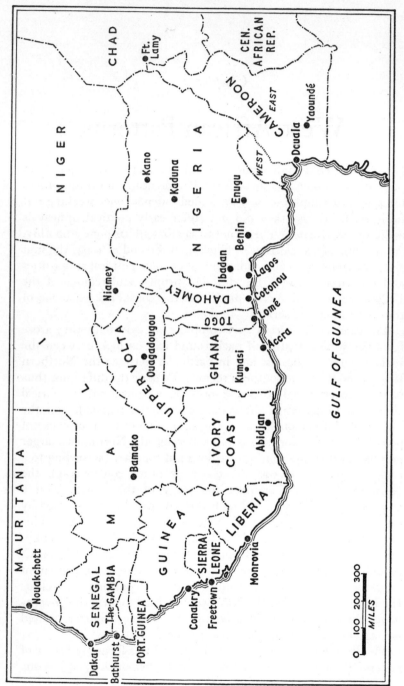

I. WEST AFRICA

of the earliest leaders of the Nigerian independence movement, a man of immense prestige and influence. He hesitated. He obviously objected to the election result, and his sympathies, not surprisingly, seemed to be on the side of the NCNC, who wished to have the election declared null and void. For a day or so, it appeared likely that President Azikiwe would refuse to call Sir Abubakar. The text of a broadcast by the President was already in the hands of the press.

In fact the crisis passed, after much talk behind the scenes, and a quiet show of strength by Sir Abubakar. The President-a constitutional and ceremonial head of state, without executive powers such as President Nkrumah possessed-called on him to form a government. Sir Abubakar for his part announced his intention of giving his administration as broad a national base as possible. Nigeria survived that major test, with the settlement of a political quarrel by a compromise rather than by a civil war. Much of the credit for the settlement was due to the leading figures in the controversy-Sir Abubakar, whose calmness and personal authority marked him out as one of the great leaders of Africa and whose death in January 1966 was a great loss to the continent, and Dr. Azikiwe who, having accepted the political limitations of the office of non-executive president, decided, when he could have tried to seize power, to stand by the constitutional rules.

In January 1966, tragically, the apparent stability and cohesion of Nigeria were shaken by a military *coup d'état*-a phenomenon by no means uncommon in neighbouring countries but one which came as a shock and a surprise to those who know Nigeria.

The 1964 crisis and that of January 1966-itself the culmination of months of ill-feeling and strife-underline the fact that the political realities of Nigeria are not at all comparable with those of the United Kingdom.

One of the most important political issues-the balance of power between the peoples of the different regions, and the related question of the census-is important simply because of the structure and composition of Nigeria. It is inconceivable, for example, that census figures should be a cause of bitter controversy in a British election.

If the political background is different, so is the structure of the political machine. Of course, as part of the colonial legacy there are many superficial similarities. In the early part of 1964, I was in Lagos for the visit of the then British Prime Minister, Sir Alec Douglas-Home. One of the features of his short visit was a speech which he gave to a joint meeting of the upper and lower houses of the federal legislature, and as the journalists sat in the public gallery of the well-appointed parliament building, listening to the closing stages of a debate on Lagos affairs while waiting for the Senate to join the lower house, and welcome Sir Alec, we had only the magnificent spectrum of colourful national dress (and surroundings far more modern than the Palace of Westminster) to remind us that this was Lagos, not London. The politenesses, the formalities, the jokes were those of the Mother of Parliaments. In Nigeria, as in Ghana, the trappings and trimmings of Parliament like those of the High Court are inherited. The problems and preoccupations of M.P.s, however, are an indigenous growth.

So, frankly, are the weaknesses of the Nigerian system. Above all, there is a tradition of corruption that is certainly not a uniquely Nigerian characteristic, but which reaches a formidable peak in Nigeria. Many politicians have their price. Industrialists often find it expedient to line the pockets of those in authority if they want to be sure of a particular contract. To an outside observer, one of the most depressing, and potentially dangerous, features of Nigerian society (as of other developing countries) is the wide disparity that exists between the haves and the have-nots, the privileged and the poor. It is particularly noticeable in Lagos, where the flashy ministerial limousine can easily cost more to maintain in a month than the bedroom steward in your hotel (who has a wife and two children to support) earns in the same period. And he is lucky to have a job at all.

Another major defect of the 'pre-coup' Nigerian system was inefficiency. Jokingly, people said that you could glean more information about what was going on by spending three hours round noon on Saturday in the Island Club, than could be obtained by a series of assiduous official calls during the working week, simply because so many of the people you tried to see did not keep the appointment, or were not in their offices, or knew nothing about the subject even when they could be found. It is a joke which contains more than a germ of truth. The Nigerian administration does not run so smoothly as the Ghanaian. The most able and experienced Nigerian civil servants carry far too heavy a load, because there are far too few of them.

Given ideal conditions, there are many ways in which the system could be streamlined. But although conditions are not ideal, and although, in consequence, even the friendliest critic can find dozens of faults and weaknesses in the system, it has a resilience which derives from the existence of a fairly adequate reservoir of trained manpower. Nigeria has judges with long experience at the bar, army officers who have not only been trained but have had an opportunity to put their training into practice before being left on their own, university graduates who have held responsible positions in the Civil Service before being subjected to the peculiar pressures of independent Africa – pressures far removed from those to be found in the strong and confident British Civil Service on which their own is modelled. Certainly by British standards the administrative resources of Nigeria are meagre, but it would be a mistake to judge Nigeria – or any other African country – by British standards. The services provided by the Nigerian Government are necessarily far less sophisticated than those provided in Britain; Nigeria is, after all, an underdeveloped country. The relevant question to ask is: are the services adequate?

Until the end of 1965, at least, events suggested that they were. Nigeria had held together, surviving quite serious strains, and the government machine had been able to withstand a number of shocks. As I write, the events of January 1966 throw the future into doubt, and it is not clear whether the country will survive in anything like its old form. It will not be clear for some time, until the new pattern has had time to emerge. If I may risk a prediction, it is that in spite of the coup, a traumatic experience whose effects will surely be felt for a long time, the natural resilience of the Nigerian people will once again produce a compromise, though it will necessarily this time be a compromise with grim and macabre overtones.

In assessing whether my prediction, and my view of developments from independence until January 1966, are valid, it is worth noting that the strains to which the administration has been subjected have not been simply domestic. As the most important state of tropical Africa, the Federation of Nigeria has been called upon to play an important role, a role of leadership, in international affairs. She has had to back up her policies and beliefs by action, particularly in the Congo, and she has met the challenge with distinction. The Nigerian police contingent in the Congo won general

c

acclaim, and it was certainly, for long periods, the only effective force of law and order in Leopoldville. The Nigerian army, too, though only a small force, accepted a heavy commitment of contribution to the United Nations military force in the Congo, and discharged it with distinction. I saw something of the Nigerian army in these difficult conditions. They were a well-disciplined, well-turned-out body whose officers were always conscious of their role as supporters of the legal government rather than as an army of occupation–not an easy role to play in a country where, at the time, the legal government was incompetent, and totally unable to maintain any effective control.

Nigeria has also been in a position to provide technical aid to fellow African states on a bilateral basis. The most obvious occasion occurred after the army mutinies in East Africa early in 1964. Then the Nigerian Government sent an army battalion to Tanganyika to replace British troops in maintaining law and order while the mutinous Tanganyikan Army was being reorganized. There are numerous cases of individual Nigerians (and Ghanaians also) who hold important posts in other countries–judges and magistrates in particular.

One could cynically argue that this sort of technical assistance is fairly easy, for countries which have for long produced large numbers of lawyers, but precious few agricultural experts or engineers. There is something in this, and it is true that the educational systems of the former British West African countries have concentrated on producing only certain categories of educated men and women. As Ken Post points out in his book *The New States of West Africa**:

Although the number of West African university students is increasing, the manpower planner must be concerned at the distribution of their subjects. Africa's primary need is for doctors, engineers, scientists, and agricultural experts, not for lawyers and literary critics.

One of the pressing problems currently facing the Nigerian Governments (federal and regional) is the growing number of educated, unemployed, young people who, having studied at a university, are no longer prepared to till the soil or do any but prestigious white-collar jobs–which do not exist in sufficient numbers to absorb them.

* Penguin African Library, 1963.

Nevertheless, serious though this problem is, it is not to be compared in gravity with the dearth of talent in other parts of Africa. Shortly before its independence, for example, Malawi (then Nyasaland) had, not an excess of lawyers, but just one African qualified barrister (Orton Chirwa, who became Attorney-General, but was soon dismissed in the Malawi cabinet crisis of 1964).

Political realities in Nigeria (or in Ghana or in Sierra Leone), as I have emphasized, are totally different from those in the United Kingdom. The basis of power is different. The legacy of colonial rule is certainly not a political system, nor a set of ideological guidelines. The most striking similarities with the British system are the superficial ones–the Speaker's wig, the Parliamentary jokes. What has been left by the colonial rulers is the–most important–leaven of educated people, and people who had time before independence to acquire practical experience in the business of running a modern state. That this leaven exists is due to a number of causes. Education was taken seriously in West Africa at a fairly early stage (Achimota College in Ghana was founded in 1924. Fourah Bay College took in its first students in 1827, and was affiliated to Durham University in 1876). West Africa was never suitable climatically for white settlement and so there never grew up the feeling that the West African countries were destined to become white man's domains. It is true that projects were drawn up around the end of the eighteenth century for settlement of Sierra Leone by Europeans.* They proved to be quite impracticable, and in any case, this was a century before the colonial era proper began. By the end of the nineteenth century, no one seriously advocated European permanent settlement in West Africa. The administrators, the traders who worked there never wanted to make it their permanent home. Added to these conditions was the fact that independence came to West Africa far more gradually than to the rest of the continent and the preparations were therefore much more thorough.

Ghana's constitutional development we have already considered. Sierra Leone acquired by Order in Council in 1951 a Legislative Council of thirty-two members of whom seven were *ex officio*, seven were elected from the Colony, twelve were elected from the Protectorate by the Protectorate District Councils, two were elected

* For an interesting discussion of these schemes, see Philip Curtin, *The Image of Africa*, Macmillan, 1965.

from the Protectorate Assembly and two were nominated by the Governor.

This was not a particularly advanced constitution, and it still left a formally recognized cleavage between the Colony (the Freetown Peninsula, a colony since 1808) and the far less developed and less sophisticated Protectorate inland–the 'up-country' regions. Two years later, however, in 1953, the ministerial system was introduced–that is to say, elected members of the legislature assumed responsibility, as ministers, for particular aspects of the work of government. In 1954, the system was further sophisticated by the appointment of a Chief Minister (Dr., later Sir Milton, Margai). This post went, automatically, to the leader of the majority party in the legislature.

In 1956 the Legislative Council was enlarged, under a new constitution, and it changed its name, becoming the House of Representatives. In its new form it consisted of a Speaker, four *ex officio* members, fifty-one elected members, two nominated members (who had no vote). An election was fought in 1957 under this new constitution, and pretty well all adult men, and a good number of adult women, had the vote. The separation of Colony and Protectorate was no longer reflected in the constitution.

Constitutional development was carried a step further in 1958 by the exclusion from the Executive Council–that is to say, the government–and from the House of Representatives, of the *ex officio* members. The Executive Council from then on consisted of elected ministers, and their chairman, formerly known as Chief Minister, became Prime Minister. Sir Milton Margai still held the office.

In nearly every respect, Sierra Leone was independent. The limitations on independence were formalities–the continuing legal responsibility of the British Government for such things as external affairs, and the theoretical power to suspend the constitution. For two more years the country continued under this system, and then in London in the spring of 1960 a final constitutional conference took place to agree the changes necessary in any 'internal self-government' constitution to convert it to the constitution for full independence. The country became independent in April 1961. As I write, the Prime Minister is Sir Albert Margai, brother of the late Sir Milton, whom he succeeded.

This brief outline of the recent constitutional development of

Sierra Leone, like that of Ghana and Nigeria, follows a pattern that became common in the next few years of colonial unravelling. It can be summed up as progress from total colonial rule, by a Governor representing the British Government, through the appointment of local advisors, then the election of some form of local council, leading to the election of a legislature with limited powers. The legislature's powers are gradually increased; members of the legislature undertake some of the work and responsibility of government; the powers actually exercised by the British Government are steadily reduced until they exist only on paper. Finally, even the paper powers go, and the apron strings (or perhaps one should say the umbilical cord) attaching the colony to Whitehall, are severed. Full independence has come.

The pattern, as I say, is now familiar. To those of us who were covering colonial affairs in 1961 and 1962, vintage years for the writing of independence constitutions, it is familiar to the point of boredom. What distinguishes the West African territories we have been considering from the East and Central African ones is not the framework of constitutional development, but the speed at which it took place.

Ghana and Sierra Leone, as we can see, followed each constitutional advance by a period of consolidation. The same is true of Nigeria, where the whole process was complicated and delayed by the fact that Nigeria is a federation whose parts had different ideas and had reached different stages of sophistication. Nigeria had elected members in its legislature, though admittedly few, under the 1922 constitution, but the real advance, in modern terms, began in 1947, with the setting up of both regional and central assemblies. There was further, major, advance in 1951, but the 1951 constitution worked badly, and in 1953, after a crisis, a series of conferences began and resulted, in 1954, in the first constitution formally asserting that the country was a Federation. There were further constitutional discussions in 1957 and 1958. The regions (then three) achieved internal self-government in 1957 (Eastern Nigeria and Western Nigeria) and 1959 (Northern Nigeria). In 1959 there was an election to the Federal House of Representatives, and the House at its first meeting early in 1960 passed a resolution asking the British Government to grant independence from October 1. This procedure had been agreed at the final discussions in 1958, and independence came as requested.

By comparison with India, the pace was fast. By comparison with India, the West African countries were under-developed in terms of administration, and of numbers of local people with education and experience. But these West African countries did have a reasonable number of such people, and the process of constitutional development was sufficient to give both ministers and officials a fair idea of the techniques and difficulties of running a modern state.

In discussing Ghana, I suggested that the many things that could be criticized there were largely things that had nothing to do with the behaviour of the colonial power before independence. They were things that arose, for example, from the ideological attitude, and the behaviour, of the government, and these are things which in an independent state no outsider can or should control. Similarly in this discussion of Nigeria and Sierra Leone I do not wish to imply that everything is perfect, that all is running smoothly and that nothing can go wrong. Indeed, I have already indicated that the administrative machine runs far from smoothly and that a great many things have gone wrong.

Certain possibilities of trouble are obvious to any reasonably well-informed observer. In Nigeria, for instance, will hostile feelings between North and South diminish, or will they continue to fester and constitute a continuing threat to the unity of the country? Can Nigeria cope with great economic difficulties, and get the right sort of industrial development, the right sort of modernized farming, under way, given its overstrained and under-trained civil service (and its unhealthily widespread corruption)? In Sierra Leone, will the Government succeed in launching the country economically, or will it simply stagnate?

Some people would give optimistic answers to these questions, some pessimistic. It is not my intention to give any answers at all, since the questions, I maintain, are not relevant to my subject. My point is quite simple. The steps taken by the British Government to prepare these countries for independence, though not ideal, were adequate. If you teach a child to swim the breast-stroke, he will not necessarily become an Olympic champion, or even get along very fast in the water, but if, having taught him, you throw him in at the deep end of the swimming pool, you do so on the reasonable assumption that he will be able to keep afloat. That seems a fair analogy for these countries and their preparation for independence. Unfortunately, in the case of some other territories, the swimming lessons have not even produced competence at the breast-stroke, and sometimes, indeed, it is as if they have been thrown into the pool with a couple of bricks round their neck.

2. CENTRAL AFRICA

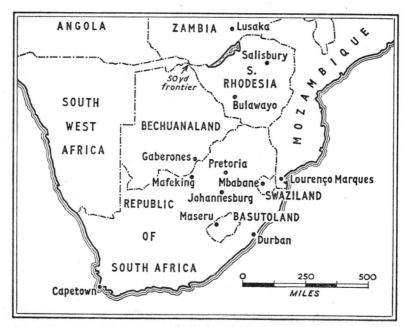

3. SOUTHERN AFRICA

Chapter 3

East and Central Africa

In November 1963 I visited Nyasaland, then only eight months away from full independence as the state of Malawi. One of the most obvious characteristics of the country was the almost total lack of African administrators at anything above the most junior level, and equally the lack of trained and qualified African magistrates.

Politically, it was naturally desirable for Dr. Banda's Government to appoint Africans to key posts, and in following this policy, Dr. Banda decided to create local courts to replace the old chiefs' courts which had long been felt to be loaded against nationalist supporters. Some of the early decisions made by the local courts were bad and manifestly unjust, and rightly attracted adverse publicity. One case, in particular, seemed to the many critics of the system to prove what they were saying. It concerned a Dane who had appeared in court to give evidence, and was summarily convicted of an offence with which he had not been charged, and hauled off to prison.

At the time of my visit, Europeans in Nyasaland tended to cite this and other examples as indications that life under Dr. Banda would cease to be worth living after independence. Amid all the gloomy predictions, people were apt to forget that the Dane had been immediately released, that the Minister of Justice (Mr. Orton Chirwa) had been emphasizing to local court presidents the need to be completely fair and to tell convicted people of their right to appeal, and that the local courts' decisions were reviewed, and often upset. The system was certainly not ideal. The justice dispensed under it was rough and ready and would have caused raised eyebrows in an English town, but the defects of the system were basically those of a lack of trained men.

It is easy enough to criticize the independent (or, as it then was, nearly independent, Government of Nyasaland) for failing to maintain high legal and administrative standards. For Europeans who had lived there in the 'old days', the change was particularly deplorable, and their anxieties and criticisms were perfectly understandable.

But what was Dr. Banda to do? Like any other political leader, he has to practise the art of the possible. He has to make the best use he can of the resources, human and otherwise, at his disposal. The blunt fact is that, as independence approached, Dr. Banda had pitifully few resources to call on.

It is true that Malawi is a poor country, overcrowded and underendowed, with no known mineral wealth. It is landlocked and relies for its import and export traffic on the route through Portuguese Mozambique. Even in independence, it has relied heavily on the British taxpayer and Treasury for aid in meeting its recurrent, day-to-day expenditure (quite apart from funds for economic development), and now, after a political upheaval and a revolt by some of the country's ablest men soon after independence, it depends even more heavily than before on outsiders (mainly British) to run its essential services, military and civilian. Its inhabitants are not, however, less gifted than any other people, nor less intelligent. There is no reason to suppose that they could not be trained and educated as effectively as other people.

In fact the concentrated training of administrators (and of local court presidents) began less than two years before independence. In November 1963 only eight Africans held administrative grade posts in the Nyasaland Civil Service, out of a total of 116 in that grade. At the Mpemba Institute near Blantyre, eight months before independence, crash courses were in progress, under the direction of Mr. M. J. Bennion, enthusiastically adapting to the conditions of Nyasaland the lessons he had learnt while running the School of Public Administration at Zaria, Northern Nigeria. Administrative officers were doing a nine-month course designed to provide them with a basic groundwork of knowledge. In general, their initial educational standard was low. On finishing the Mpemba course most of them would be thrown in at the deep end, into senior responsible posts. The training they were receiving, excellent in its way, was hardly ideal. The whole system of crash courses of this kind was a makeshift.

Why was it necessary? The glib answer is that Nyasaland (and Kenya, and any other country you care to name) were not ready for independence, and should not therefore have got it when they did. It is an answer which does not stand up to examination. If you accept, as I do, the theory of the pressure of history, the inexorable path of events, you will accept that independence might have been delayed by a month or so, but not by any long period – except of course by military might, which would have been a sterile and unreasonable policy.

It is possible to argue against this view of the situation, but significantly the British Government implicitly accepted it. In 1959 Dr. Banda, recently returned to Nyasaland after forty years away, many of them practising medicine in London, had established himself as a national leader dedicated to destroying 'this stupid federation' (the Federation of Rhodesia and Nyasaland), and to gaining for his country independence on her own. He made no secret of his views. He expressed them clearly on many occasions. Following disturbances, the (colonial) Government declared a state of emergency in March 1959 and Dr. Banda himself was detained in a Southern Rhodesian prison.

A year later, to the annoyance of Sir Roy Welensky, the Federal Prime Minister, and his colleagues, Mr. Iain Macleod, then British Colonial Secretary, arranged for Dr. Banda's release and return to Nyasaland, where the two men met.

That was the background to the constitutional conference which took place in London in July 1960, at which the framework of a new constitution was agreed. It provided for the first time for the direct election of Africans to the legislature, with a qualitative franchise on upper and lower electoral rolls. It was seen, rightly, by Dr. Banda as the means of putting a majority of Africans into the legislature. That, quite clearly, was also the understanding of Mr. Macleod and his Colonial Office advisors.

Acceptance of the inevitability, and imminence, of African rule, however, was not accompanied in East and Central Africa by an adequate appreciation of what was implied by acceptance. In the East and Central African countries the administrative machine, on the eve and the morrow of independence, was far weaker than it had been in the West African countries, and the efforts that had been made to strengthen it were too little and too late.

Even more serious than the shortage of administrators was the lack of technically and professionally qualified men. On February 1, 1962, Mr. William Clark, Director of the Overseas Development Institute, discussed this problem in a lecture to a joint

meeting of the Royal African Society and the Royal Commonwealth Society.* He said:

The criticism that can be made of the colonial past is that the training
of African vets and agricultural officers, and engineers and so on was
left till far too late. It really only began in the last few years, so that now
if British technicians leave, as seems likely, in 1962–64, there will be a
gap of two or three years before African trainees finish their courses
and can even begin to take over.

Mr. Clark suggested various ways of reducing the effect of this
crisis of manpower. One of the most obvious—which would have
been also one of the most effective—was that the Government of
the day should change its mind and reconsider its persistent refusal
to establish 'some sort of Commonwealth Service which would
continue after the imminent end of our Colonial Empire'. Such a
service, providing a proper career for the technical men, the agri-
culturalists, the engineers, who could be sent, on temporary
assignments to those parts of the world where they were most
needed, would have been a sensible way of retaining experienced
men whose overseas careers would otherwise be abruptly and
prematurely terminated, and at the same time providing help of the
kind and at the time when it was most needed. The French
adopted, successfully, a similar arrangement. French teachers, and
experts and administrators, are still to be found, in the independent
French-speaking territories but with their careers guaranteed by
France.

In 1960 the Select Committee on Estimates of the House of
Commons had recommended precisely this—the creation of a
Commonwealth technical and advisory service whose officers
would serve overseas but would remain in the British Government's employ. In July 1961 the Department of Technical Cooperation was set up (the forerunner of the present Ministry of
Overseas Development). It was the obvious body to sponsor and
coordinate such a service. In fact, after just under a year of
existence, it produced a White Paper† underlining the Government's refusal to take the step. In this it was agreed that the idea
was superficially attractive but argued that it would be impractic-

* *After Independence In East Africa*, Overseas Development Institute
Occasional Paper No. 1.
† *Recruitment for Service Overseas: Future Policy*, Cmnd 1740.

able because the British Government would have no control over the number, duration and type of vacancies to be filled and because, with the probability of periods of unemployment between appointments, such a service would not attract people of the quality required.

This was, to put it mildly, a defeatist argument, and illustrated a failure to grasp the essentials of the task still facing Britain as she adapted her colonial policies to changing conditions. When one looks at the alternative that was in fact accepted, the refusal to create a career service seems even more obtuse. The alternative was the perpetuation of the compensation scheme introduced with India's independence in 1947. Under it, newly independent countries are expected to pay large sums in compensation for loss of office to British civil servants who lose their careers when the régime changes. The East African countries did not possess the necessary funds, and so Britain herself made large grants and loans to enable the compensation payments to be made. In any case, the attitude of nationalist politicians, however realistic, does not usually include enthusiasm and gratitude for years of colonial domination.

Those colonial servants who have spent many years in a territory have been able to leave on independence with a substantial lump sum. The newly independent country, having lost its qualified men has had to seek others on contract—sometimes taking the old ones back on different terms of service. The British taxpayer, having subsidized the compensation scheme, has also had to subsidize the provision of substitute experts. The compensation system itself has been a cause of ill-will between Britain and her former colonies at the moment of independence. In short, the whole system has every possible disadvantage.

In August 1965 the Ministry of Overseas Development published a report on its work (Cmnd 2736) in which the failure of the previous policy was tacitly acknowledged. It was announced that:

where specialist staff is required for key posts the supply can be ensured only by creating additional capacity in home establishments . . . A total of at least 400 posts will be added for this purpose to home establishments in government departments, universities, technical colleges, etc. . . . the aim will be to build up the numbers to at least 400 in two to three years and the fullest use will be made of those who have already had experience overseas, as well as of young men and women with suitable qualifications. The professions which we aim to cover in this way include agriculture, forestry, animal health, economics, statistics, educational administration, law, public administration, engineering, architecture, town planning, land survey and geology.

The East and Central African countries were not all, of course, in quite the same parlous state as Malawi, nor were their problems quite the same. Tanganyika, for example, was not a colony but a United Nations Trust territory (formerly a League of Nations mandated territory) administered by Britain as the trustee power. Like its neighbours, however, Tanganyika entered independence with serious difficulties or potential difficulties unsolved. In fact they burst into the open at the beginning of 1964 when the army mutinied and order was restored only with the aid of British troops, asked for by the Tanganyikan Government. There were specific political causes of this upheaval, but basically it was able to occur because of a lack of properly trained and experienced indigenous army officers–a deficiency true also of Kenya and Uganda, to which the mutiny spread (to be quelled by prompt and firm actions by Mr. Kenyatta and Dr. Obote, supported, like the Tanganyikans, by British troops). The East African mutinies came immediately after the *coup d'état* in Zanzibar, which, one month after the granting of independence by Britain, overthrew the Sultan's Government, formed round the traditional minority Arab ruling class. Zanzibar is a particularly depressing example of the failure of British colonial policy.

The existence of serious racial tensions between the Arabs and the Africans and Afro-Shirazis on the island was well known to the British Government. The Zanzibar general election of June 1961 had provoked riots in which sixty-eight people were killed. The Commission of Inquiry which investigated the trouble concluded that racial feelings were not alone in causing the riots, but significantly they commented, 'In our view the evidence conclusively shows that the Afro-Shirazi Party made its appeal to the electorate on a racial basis, and that the Zanzibar Nationalist Party introduced religion into the controversy . . .' * Then in the spring of 1962 the Zanzibar constitutional conference in London ended in failure because agreement could not be reached on the demand of the Afro-Shirazi Party (then in opposition) for an election to be

* *Report of a Commission of Inquiry into Disturbances in Zanzibar during June, 1961*. Colonial number 353.

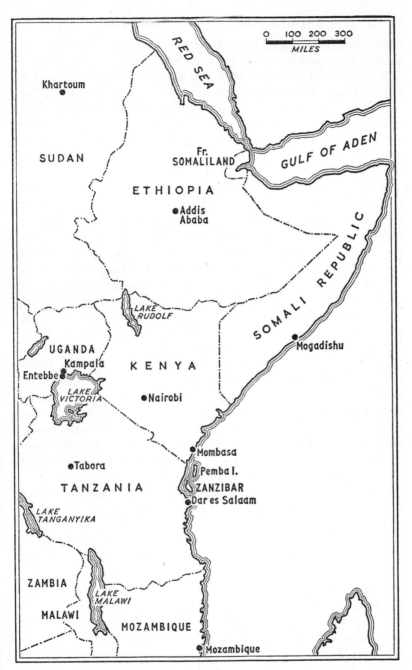

4. EAST AFRICA

held before independence. In the event, the revolution removed the need for the election that did not take place.

It would be foolish to suggest that anyone could have predicted precisely what would happen after independence in Zanzibar. The revolution was a surprise. The circumstances which allowed revolution to breed, however, were so well known that the British Government's failure to attempt to improve the situation before launching the island into sovereign statehood was a clear case of irresponsibility.

If this seems to be a harsh view, the British Government's behaviour after the Zanzibar revolution lends weight to it. At that time, with chaotic conditions on the island, it fairly soon became obvious that whatever its weaknesses and its incompetence, the revolutionary régime was there to stay. In so far as anyone was in control, it was the revolutionaries. What had happened was not –it still is not–a happy example of the decolonization process at work. Zanzibar is obviously not the sort of example which defenders of the British colonial record would choose to cite. Like it or not, however, the facts had to be faced, and in facing them the British Government had one great advantage over everyone else. It was the presence in Zanzibar of a British mission under Mr. Crosthwait, arrived not long before to take up his post as High Commissioner to the newly independent State. By normal diplomatic procedure, his official status changed automatically with the revolution because the British Government had, of course, diplomatically recognized the Sultan's Government. In practice, Mr. Crosthwait was accorded by the *de facto* revolutionary government the privileges of a *de facto* diplomatic representative, and as a result of this treatment, he was able to do a certain amount to ease the lot of British subjects caught in the mess.

The revolution took place on Sunday, January 12. Within a few days its outcome was certain. Indeed, on that very Sunday Mr. Sandys, Secretary of State for Commonwealth Relations, had wisely taken the decision not to send British troops to support the Sultan's Government (under the Prime Minister Shaikh Muhammad Shamte Hamadi), quoting in a public statement a report from the British High Commissioner to the effect that the Zanzibar Government had lost control of the situation. The British Government, in short, recognized the fact that the revolution had succeeded. Under British practice, diplomatic recognition is normally granted to a government which is established in power–since recognition expresses neither liking nor approval. Other Commonwealth countries, and the British press, urged the Government in this case to recognize the new Zanzibar régime. On February 12, a month after the coup, there was a report that West Germany had decided to give recognition (relations with Germany were later confused by Zanzibar's flirtation with East Germany). Still the Commonwealth Relations Office had to report only that the matter was under consideration. On February 20, the Zanzibar Government finally lost patience, and expelled Mr. Crosthwait. After thus earning the maximum ill-will from the Zanzibar revolutionaries, the British Government compounded its folly three days later by recognizing the new régime on February 23. Mr. Crosthwait was put in the invidious position of having to creep back to his post and begin to reshape relations from scratch.

However it is explained, policy on Zanzibar was ill-conceived. Indeed, there was really no policy at all, but a series of random reactions to events.

What is the explanation of Britain's failure, in East and Central Africa, to make adequate preparations for independence, even when it had become politically inevitable? Probably the underlying reason was that these areas were traditionally seen as white man's country–or in the case of Tanganyika, Uganda and Malawi, where white settlers were not numerically important, appendages to white man's country.

Mr. Tom Mboya, one of the leading Kenya Ministers and for many years one of the best known and ablest Kenya politicians, tells a story in his book *Freedom and After** about the time when he, newly qualified as a sanitary inspector of the Nairobi City Council, came up against racial prejudice of an extraordinary kind. A European woman came into the laboratory with a bottled sample of milk for testing.

'Good morning, madam,' I said.

When I spoke, she turned round and asked, 'Is there anybody here?'

I was a bit shocked and angry, but decided her question was quite amusing. So I asked, 'Is there something wrong with your eyes?'

It is a vivid commentary on the socio-racial superiority of the European which was the hallmark of Kenya society until almost

* André Deutsch Ltd., 1965.

D

the very eve of independence. In Kenya, the political dominance of the white man was bound up with the question of land. Tribal ownership of land, particularly among the Kikuyu, the dominant tribe of Kenya, is a matter of deep and fervent feeling, akin to the typical Englishman's feeling for his right to privacy in his home. Much of the best farming land of Kenya, the White Highlands as they were then known, was in white hands, quite legally and with the support and encouragement of the British Government. This situation could not fail to provide a bone of contention that inevitably grew more serious as political awareness among Africans increased. John Hatch, in his *A History of Postwar Africa*,* wrote: 'That the British colonial government had confirmed this white ownership by legislation and even prevented Africans from being employed as farm managers in the white highlands, only identified the British with this racial policy.' Eventually, the fact that white farmers would be dispossessed came to be accepted as one of the political facts of Kenya life–and the British Government had to agree to pay enormous sums of compensation in the resettlement schemes.

But acceptance of the realities of the land question, and recognition that East and Central Africa could not continue to be thought of as white man's territory, came slowly and painfully. In Southern Rhodesia, it has not come yet. When it came, there was an appreciable time lag between on the one hand acceptance of the inevitable and the decision to act on it politically and on the other a readiness to change the structure of society–at least of 'official' society–which must accompany the political change. In Central Africa, the matter was complicated further by the hesitant, not to say pusillanimous, behaviour of the British Government in its dealings with the Rhodesian Federal Government.

I want now to examine in more detail recent colonial policy in three territories–Kenya, Uganda and Zambia (Northern Rhodesia) –each of which illustrates in a different way a more or less serious failure by Britain to live up to the standards expected of a responsible colonial power.

* André Deutsch Ltd., 1965.

Chapter 4

Kenya, Mr Macleod's First Task

TOM MBOYA'S story reproduced in the previous chapter is symptomatic of the pattern of Kenya society until shortly before independence–certainly until the late 1950s. Kenya was a white man's country. Economic power was firmly in white hands. Kenya farmers, many of them ex-service men who had gone to the colony with the blessing and encouragement of successive British governments, were the backbone of the economy and over the years had developed well and profitably the magnificent agricultural potential of a country where almost everything grows, at some altitude throughout the year.

The white settlers had not succeeded in getting for themselves the degree of political power that they would have liked. In the period after the Second World War they had to accept a series of constitutional changes which increased the representation in the legislature of non-Europeans (Africans, Asians and Arabs). Nevertheless, as they examined the statements and attitudes of British governments over the years it is not surprising that they drew the conclusion that their adopted country was to remain in white hands indefinitely. Looking back over the past few years it seems extraordinary that any body of intelligent people could have thought in this way–but there was after all no reason why the settler community should shew a greater perception than the British Government. The really incredible thing is that even two years after Ghana had become independent official as well as settler attitudes were based on the tacit assumption that Kenya could remain in some unexplainable way an oasis by-passed by the wind of change.

Quite recently I was talking to a young member of the Overseas Civil Service (the new name for the Colonial Service), who had joined it on going down from Oxford in 1957–and eight years later, as a man of 31, has had to shape a new career for himself when his chosen one folded beneath him. He told me that, at his

47

initial training course before taking up his first post in the Kenya administration, he and his fellow students were assured that East Africa's 'colonial' future could be measured in decades. When, in August 1959, Mr. Julius Nyerere predicted that Tanganyika would have self-government within five years and independence within ten at most, he was thought quite unrealistic. A little later in the same year, at a conference of Pafmeca (the Pan-African Freedom Movement for East and Central Africa), he found it necessary to correct reports that he had been calling for full independence by the end of 1960, explaining that he was talking about responsible government, which would be an interim stage on the road to independence. Yet when Tanganyika actually became fully independent in December 1961, no one found the fact surprising.

Indeed, with Ghana independent in 1957, and Nigeria's approach to that status already gathering momentum, it should have been far clearer than it was that East Africa, though more backward and therefore likely to move more slowly, could not be held for long as a white bastion. As far back as 1923 the British Government, in a White Paper known as the Devonshire Declaration (after the then Colonial Secretary, the Duke of Devonshire), had proclaimed 'Primarily Kenya is an African territory . . . the interests of the African natives must be paramount.' Neither at the time, nor for many years to come, had African paramountcy meant much. It had certainly not meant African political power. Understandably, Europeans who had gone to Kenya, built themselves a livelihood in a beautiful country and enjoyed every encouragement from Westminster, were loth even to consider handing over Kenya lock, stock and barrel to Africans whom many of them saw only as servants and farm workers–excellent people, to be treated well but paternally. Add to this natural unwillingness to give up the advantages of a privileged status the revulsion which most Europeans who had lived through it felt for the Mau Mau tragedy of the 1950s, and it is easy to see why the atmosphere in Kenya was quite different from that in Ghana or Nigeria. What was understandable for the Kenya settlers, however, was far less excusable in the Colonial Office and the Cabinet room. It did not require great political acumen to see that Kenya was irrevocably launched along the same road as Ghana and Nigeria. It should have been clear that Mau Mau, for all its bestiality, was an outbreak of nationalism in an acute form, and that the clock could never be put back again.

These things should have been clear but they were not-or at least, they were not seen as phenomena demanding urgent and inspired action-until the moment in 1959 when Mr. Harold Macmillan, who had been returned to office at the October election, decided to change Britain's colonial policy, and appointed Mr. Iain Macleod as Secretary of State for the Colonies to implement it.

Kenya was the first big problem facing the new Secretary of State, and it was a symbolic setting for the change of policy which the 1959 Conservative Government introduced, throwing over in the process many of the hitherto accepted Conservative dogmas.

Early in 1960 Mr. Macleod presided over his first big colonial constitutional conference at Lancaster House-the Kenya conference. While it was in progress, Mr. Macmillan the Prime Minister, was journeying round Africa on his famous 'wind of change' tour. It is sometimes assumed that Mr. Macmillan invented, or created, the wind of change, the implication being that if he had said nothing, all would have gone on smoothly as before. In fact, of course, he was simply recognizing publicly what was rapidly becoming impossible to miss. In trimming her sails before the wind, Britain was only being realistic, and there are good grounds for accepting that this adoption of realism (or ignominious retreat, as the Conservative right-wingers would have it) in colonial policy had been decided on as the new Conservative Government came to power. This is certainly the view of Sir Michael Blundell, who played an important catalystic role in Kenya's transition from white domination to black independence, and drew to himself in the process much unpopularity among his fellow-Europeans, most of whom were less far-sighted than he. In his autobiography, *So Rough a Wind*,* he wrote, 'Whatever history may record as the actual facts, a dramatic change was to take place in the policy of the British Government after the general election in October 1959 . . . the decision was taken to withdraw from Africa as quickly as decency would permit.' Among the influences which led to this 'complete reversal of former decisions and long-term plans', Sir Michael mentions the fact that 'The affluent society which was evident over almost all Europe and the colossal effort

* Weidenfeld and Nicolson, 1964.

of post-war reconstruction had made European electorates inward-looking and disinclined to get involved in awkward and often unrewarding issues further afield.'

That is a negative interpretation, and it is not one that I find wholly satisfying. There were other more important factors which contributed to Britain's change of heart. Dame Margery Perham listed some in her 1965 B.B.C. talks *Thinking Aloud about Africa*.

There was the Mau Mau rebellion and its culmination in the Hola Camp incident in which eleven Mau Mau detainees died as a result of ill-treatment by camp officials. There was the return to Nyasaland of Dr. Banda and the subsequent 1959 riots and shootings. There was the report on these riots by the Devlin Commission (Cmnd 814), which recorded that the supremely important cause for the Africans of Nyasaland was political freedom.

In a famous passage, Lord Devlin and his fellow-commissioners commented:

Nyasaland is—no doubt only temporarily—a police state, where it is not safe for anyone to express approval of the policies of the Congress party [Dr. Banda's Malawi Congress Party] and where it is unwise to express any but the most restrained criticism of Government policy.

The Commission found in Nyasaland a widespread opposition to the Federation of Rhodesia and Nyasaland, and poured scorn on the Nyasaland (colonial) Government's view that nationalist aspirations were the thoughts of only a small minority of political Africans, mainly self seekers, and that the majority of the people were indifferent to the issue. 'We have not found this to be so,' the Commission reported. 'Even among the chiefs, many of whom are loyal to the Government and dislike Congress methods, we have not heard of a single one who is in favour of federation.'

The former British Government (also Conservative, but before the 1959 election) having appointed the Devlin Commission, repudiated its findings in a shameful exercise in electoral expediency, but as Dr. Perham pointed out in her broadcast, the British Government had to choose between shooting and . . . what? 'The Africans now had already guessed the answer. Gradualism was out. For the eastern and central African states there was to be no time for further preparation, no stages of advance. A few quick strides in the early 'sixties and—independence, now!'

It is true, of course, as Sir Michael Blundell says, that Britain's change of policy was a reversal, but it was a reversal undertaken in an acceptance of rapidly changing facts.

In my own dealings, as a journalist, with Mr. Macleod during his time as Colonial Secretary, I certainly had the feeling that he genuinely, indeed passionately, believed in what he was doing, and felt it not only the expedient course but the right one. He was not popular in Kenya. He was heartily disliked by Sir Roy Welensky, the Prime Minister of the Rhodesia and Nyasaland Federation. He was bitterly resented by influential sections of the Conservative Party. None of these reactions was surprising. On the other hand, most of the serious journalists covering the colonial events of 1960 and 1961, and trying to see things objectively, recognized in Mr. Macleod a man whose actions were based on belief to a degree which not only cynics would admit is rare among politicians. Under his two successors, Mr. Maudling and Mr. Sandys, the lines of policy were not nearly so firmly drawn and adhered to. In my view, however, Iain Macleod will be credited by future historians with being not only the Minister who implemented the Cabinet's 'wind of change' policy, but, far more significantly, the man who did more than probably anyone else to try and ensure for the white minorities of Africa some kind of a place for the future, when African rule had become a reality. It is all the more regrettable, therefore, that he allowed his reputation to be tarnished by his weak and equivocal attitude in the autumn of 1965 to the illegal declaration of independence by the Smith régime in Southern Rhodesia.

Mr. Macleod himself, in an article in the *Weekend Telegraph* (the *Daily Telegraph's* colour supplement) on March 12, 1965, explained that the 'wind of change' speech of Mr. Macmillan was not the announcement of a dramatic Cabinet decision, but a comment on a situation in which the tempo had accelerated as a result of 'a score of different deliberate decisions'. The Hola Camp tragedy, he suggested, was decisive, even more than the Nyasaland emergency. In his article Mr. Macleod wrote that the logic of the transfer of power in West Africa was that the same transfer must come 'swiftly in East and steadily in Central Africa' and could not long be delayed only because of the presence of European settlers. Referring to 1960 and 1961 as the turbulent years, he agrees that by them (and by the answer to the problem of Southern Rhodesia) 'we [presumably Britain rather than the Conservative Party] will be judged.' As a politician he had the advantage of a cold and analytical mind. He could see not only the general direction in which events were moving, but also the deviations that would have to be made along the route in the name of political manœuvre. Those of us who watched him closely at work during this period knew that he had the measure of the colonial politicians with whom he was dealing. His disadvantage was that his efforts were often sabotaged by his enemies within his own party.

Mr. Macleod began his task of arranging the transfer of power at the 1960 Kenya conference. In a way which became commonplace at subsequent constitutional conferences, but which at that time was still novel, the gathering at Lancaster House on this occasion was marked by walk-outs, arguments on points of principle, acrimonious exchanges and a flurry of statements official and unofficial to the press. For a time, indeed, it seemed that the conference would not take place at all because of the insistence of the African delegates that Mr. Jomo Kenyatta, then still under restriction following his imprisonment at the time of Mau Mau, should be present. That difficulty was smoothed over, but a more serious one arose. It was the desire of the African parties (united, as a tactical move, during the conference) to have present at Lancaster House Mr. Peter Mbiu Koinange, a senior and experienced colleague of Mr. Kenyatta who was at the time living in Ghana, exiled from Kenya where he was held by the (colonial) Kenya Government to have been one of those responsible for Mau Mau.

The refusal to admit him to the conference room caused the Africans to boycott the opening ceremony and the impasse lasted for nearly a week. Mr. Macleod, recognizing the realities of the situation rather than its face-saving aspects, produced a compromise by issuing a blank pass, admitting to Lancaster House but not to the conference room itself, so that the African delegates could fill in on it Mr. Koinange's name.

I have dwelt on this incident because it illustrates an important point—the recognition by Mr. Macleod (and, one must presume, by the Government to which he belonged) that the future of Kenya lay with African nationalists, and that simply pretending they did not exist would not make them vanish from the scene. Looking back even these few years later, that does not seem a revolutionary idea. It was in 1960, if not revolutionary, at least a surprisingly unorthodox way of looking at the Kenya political scene.

What emerged from the 1960 conference, after all the shouting had died down, was a compromise constitution, but a compromise that paved the way to rapid political advance by Africans. The rate of advance had been speeded, but more than that, the path which Kenya was to take had been changed.

To be specific, a general election was fought in January 1961, under the new constitution, with a franchise complicated by various limitations but which nevertheless brought a large number of black Kenyans for the first time on to the voters' rolls. Some seats were reserved for racial minorities (Europeans, Asians and Arabs). In the reserved seat constituencies there were primary elections in which members of the community concerned voted to decide which of the candidates standing should go forward for the general, common roll, election later. This system caused much controversy because as things turned out many of the candidates chosen by the majority of European voters in the primary contest were not elected to the legislature, Africans on the common roll voting, in the main election, for other Europeans who were more 'progressive', or less ready to stand for white political privilege.

The really important point about the 1961 election and the constitution under which it was fought was that it gave recognition to the fact that Africans, by far the majority of the population, must be granted the political power which they were demanding with increasing fervour all over Africa, and that they must get it quickly. This constitution, emerging from the 1960 conference, was as I have said a compromise, in that it created a multi-racial framework, in which the various peoples of Kenya should co-operate, each having a specific place assured by the constitution. As we have seen in recent years, multi-racial arrangements—in which votes, and seats in a legislature, are provided for the different races as races—have not worked in Africa. This does not seem to me surprising, for it is hard to imagine why any majority group, seeing the realities of power within its grasp, should willingly forego a part of that power by accepting something less than a straight, uncomplicated universal franchise. I shall say something more about multi-racialism later, in relation to the Rhodesia and Nyasaland Federation. In Kenya, it did not last, but as a temporary expedient it did serve quite well to bridge the change from white supremacy to black.

Closely linked with this fact of Africans getting political power was the position of Jomo Kenyatta. George Bennett and Carl

Rosberg, in their perceptive book *The Kenyatta Election: Kenya 1960–1961**, firmly place this election in its true perspective as a crucial point in Kenya's contemporary history. They rightly emphasize–as their title makes plain–the dominant position of Mr. Kenyatta. (To use the Mr. at the time of the election would have provoked angry explosions from many of the British politicians and others who only three years later were saying, 'Kenyatta of course is the great stabilizing influence in East Africa.') He was still under restriction, but his release was the Africans' battle cry. The African nationalists were split into two camps, the Kenya African National Union (Kanu) and the Kenya African Democratic Union (Kadu), whose tactics on the Kenyatta question were different. No serious African politician, however, would have dreamt of questioning the importance of Kenyatta himself, or the need for his release to play an active part in Kenya's affairs.

As I have explained, Mr. Macleod at the 1960 conference had accepted this too, at least tacitly. His ruse for permitting Mr. Koinange into Lancaster House, his willingness to face a walk-out by the right-wing Europeans, the constitution which emerged from the London conference, all shewed his sensitivity to the trend of events, to the realities which were symbolized in Mr. Macmillan's 'wind of change'. Unfortunately Mr. Macleod's realism was not shared by others in high places. British Government policy in Kenya was a dismal hotch-potch of unkeepable promises, irreconcilable objectives, right to the end.

It was not simply that the necessary preparations for handing over administrative tasks to an indigenous civil service, and military command to African officers, were put in hand inexcusably late, even allowing for the hectic speed with which pressures for constitutional advance built up in East Africa. The Kenya settlers, with almost everything to lose, with their pasts and their futures committed to Kenya, had a right to demand more honest treatment, and a franker indication of the truth which they were going to have to face than the British Government gave them. The concept of Kenya as a white man's country died hard and instead of killing it with a cold douche of truth when once the decision on policy had been taken, the British Government allowed the settlers –who after all were the people who most needed to know what was afoot–to go on believing in the impossible.

* Oxford University Press, 1961.

Mr. Macleod's 1960 conference set out clearly enough to those who could read at all between the lines what the future held. The European United Party read the message, and described the Lancaster House framework as the cynical abandonment of Kenya's Europeans. Honesty demanded that the lesson should be spelt out, not between the lines but unequivocally. Comforting feelings that Parliament at Westminster would never let down its 'kith and kin', that multi-racialism was an end rather than a means, that the political and social position of the Europeans could somehow be preserved, these needed to be squashed and shewn to be no more than a dream which the British Government would be wrong to try and fulfil. The Government preferred to let the dreamers sleep on.

One of the most remarkable manifestations of this failure to think policy through to its logical conclusion was the attitude towards Mr. Kenyatta.

His shadow, as we have seen, lay over the 1960 Lancaster House conference. By the time of the 1961 election, his position had grown more important. The African parties, admittedly, were split, but Mr. Kenyatta was acknowledged by all, nominally at least, as a national figure whose release was the *sine qua non* for full co-operation.

That the average European, in Kenya and elsewhere, did not like Mr. Kenyatta was unsurprising. The excesses of Mau Mau, the bestial oaths, the murder, had been a horrifying experience still fresh in the memory. In 1960 there were disquieting signs that a form of neo-Mau Mau was growing in strength and support. Having been formally convicted for his part in Mau Mau, Jomo Kenyatta was the focus of European distaste and revulsion. His trial, in an English setting, would almost certainly not have produced a conviction. In Africa, particularly at a time of great tribal stress, evidence according to common law rules is hard to come by. I have discussed this recently with a man who was a senior administrator at the time, and he agreed that strictly speaking Kenyatta should not have been convicted 'although, of course, he was definitely guilty'. Such questions are now of academic interest rather than of practical import. What was of practical import in 1960 was that the significance of Mr. Kenyatta's powerful political standing was obscured by emotions. In judging the importance of a leader what matters is the strength of his support, not the sweetness of his smile. Leaders, in short, are not always likeable – and need not be.

Even in 1961, however, many people who should have known better, who grasped intellectually the implications of constitutional decisions that had been taken, could not conquer the emotional barrier to accepting Jomo Kenyatta as one of these implications. 'Kenyatta blindness' pervaded official Kenya. In May 1960, when the Lancaster House conference must surely have been well digested, the late Sir Patrick Renison, the Governor of Kenya, in a public statement described Jomo Kenyatta as 'the African leader to darkness and death' and said he would not be released. In May there appeared as a White Paper the Corfield Report on Mau Mau's origins and growth (Cmnd 1030). It added little to what was already known. It left open the doubts about the Kapenguria trial at which Kenyatta had been convicted. It exacerbated anti-Kenyatta feelings at a time when his re-emergence on the political scene could not be far away.

The Governor's comment and the decision to publish the Corfield Report were examples of stupidity which events soon shewed up. Less than a year after his 'darkness and death' statement, in March 1961, Sir Patrick Renison had to respond to mounting African pressure by announcing that Mr. Kenyatta would be moved nearer to Nairobi. Five months later, in August 1961, came the announcement that he was to be released. By the autumn of that year, he was visiting London, and was taking a fully active part in politics. In 1962, also, he was one of the two senior ministers in an African administration presided over by – Sir Patrick Renison.

Presumably Whitehall knew and approved each of these developments. Certainly Sir Patrick Renison remained Governor until November 1962 which could hardly have happened if he had exceeded his brief. But what was gained by shilly-shallying in this way? It encouraged the Europeans – and Africans – who feared Mr. Kenyatta to believe, wrongly, that he was a spent force. It made African cooperation more difficult to obtain than it need have been. Worst of all, it portrayed the British Government as indecisive, and indicated that the policy which today was said to be out of the question would be adopted tomorrow if people made enough fuss. This was not traditional and skilful British pragmatism. It was weakness and drift.

Chapter 5

The Complications of Kenya

THE 1961 election produced a majority for KANU. Protracted negotiations, however, failed to get them to agree to form a government until Jomo Kenyatta was released—and the Governor's decision was that his release would not be permitted until a government was working. The deadlock was eventually resolved when the minority party, KADU, agreed to take office and its leader, Mr. Ronald Ngala, accepted the post of Leader of Government Business.

He was supported by Sir Michael Blundell's New Kenya Party and some others, but even so he had a majority in the legislature only by the artificial means of the appointment of members nominated by the Governor. The British Government took steps to give other support to Mr. Ngala and his colleagues, notably, in May 1961, by promising £7,000,000 in aid for the year 1961–2 above the £7,500,000 already committed. There were other, more subtle, measures of support, as for instance the presence of Mr. Macmillan, then Prime Minister, at a reception to the Kenyan Government delegation in London for financial talks.

For his part, Mr. Ngala, a sincere and honest man, set about turning himself into a national leader, concentrating wisely on improvements to national education and setting in train at once the building of a house for Jomo Kenyatta at Kiambu—a political demonstration that KADU were at least as firmly committed as KANU to his release. In June 1961 the three East African Governments (Kenya, Tanganyika and Uganda) took part in talks in London designed to make possible the eventual formation of an East African Federation. Their immediate purpose was to transform the old East Africa High Commission into the East African Common Services Organization. Mr. Ngala, whose party was becoming increasingly attracted to the concept of federalism, fully supported this purpose, although KADU was never accepted by fellow East African political leaders as truly representative of Kenya.

57

On August 1, 1961, the Governor of Kenya, and the Colonial Secretary in the House of Commons, announced that Mr. Kenyatta was to be released finally from restriction. The circumstances leading up to this announcement were set out in a White Paper (Cmnd 1459). Gradually 'the old man' returned to normal life. Observers held their breath, wondering whether he would emerge as a truly national leader, or whether he would lend his support to one or other of the two main African parties. For a time, he appeared to be ineffective. People began to claim gleefully that he was tired and finished, and that he was no longer a political force to be reckoned with. Various moves that he made to bring the two parties together again failed. The failure was attributed by many to his lack of the qualities of national leadership. In fact, as subsequent events have shewn, the failure was due far more to tribal feelings, and above all to the fear of the smaller tribes (in KADU) of domination by the Kikuyu and the Luo.

By October 1961 this fear, combined with the continuing separation of KANU and KADU, was reflected in party policy in KADU. In that month Mr. Peter Okondo, an intelligent young Member of the Legislative Council, and Parliamentary Secretary to the Minister of Finance and Development, while in London for financial talks, announced at a press conference KADU's plan for a regional Kenya, then just launched, which was to colour all future constitutional negotiations until, and indeed after, independence. Mr. Okondo said:

In Kenya KADU has launched a campaign for Regional Authority Government as a solution to mounting fears of domination by one tribe or by a combination of a few . . . By regional government we hope to develop a constitution which will prevent the emergence of tyranny or authoritarianism and absolute rule in Kenya.

In this early form the KADU plan provided for four regions which would federate under a central government–and which would be capable of 'unlimited extension . . . to apply to Uganda, Tanganyika, Nyasaland, the Rhodesias and others that may wish to join'.

This regional scheme was put forward by KADU at constitutional talks which were taking place under the Governor's chairmanship in Nairobi. It was totally rejected by KANU, who were by this time already firmly committed to the idea of unitary government. Earlier talks between the parties under Mr. Kenyatta's chairmanship had produced only disagreement, and KADU rejected his leadership. Then at the end of October, he became formally the leader of KANU.

Early in November 1961, Mr. Kenyatta came to London, which he had not visited for many years. He came as a private citizen, in the sense that he was not a member of the legislature, but also as a party leader. He saw the Colonial Secretary and officials. He gave press conferences and appeared on television. He carried off a difficult visit with dignity that survived even the efforts of the League of Empire Loyalists who threw eggs at him, and on one occasion at a press conference in the Eccleston Hotel, the entrails of an animal (chicken or sheep) wrapped in a copy of *The Times* to the accompaniment of the cry 'Take that, you're a bloody butcher, Kenyatta.'

It is true that Mr. Kenyatta still could not, at this time, be judged a fully national leader. He was still, even in Kenya, an equivocal figure. It was obvious, however, to those who saw him on his London trip that, however mild his manner, however ready he was to nod gentle agreement to his lieutenants, who did most of the talking, Mr. Kenyatta was undoubtedly the leader of KANU. His colleagues, Asian and European as well as African, deferred naturally to him.

Soon after this, KANU, through Mr. Joseph Murumbi, its London representative, later to become Foreign Minister, took a significant step which indicated that they were beginning to think in Kenyan rather than purely party terms. They arranged, with the help of the Ariel Foundation, for an agricultural and educational survey to be made by experts headed by Mr. Arthur Gaitskell, former chairman of the Sudan Gezira Board, a member of the Royal Commission East Africa 1953-4 and of the Tanganyika Agricultural Corporation, 1955, and Mr. W. K. Phillips, an agricultural economist. This mission, invited at the moment when the date of the 1962 constitutional conference (which produced the outline independence constitution) was settled, produced a report which KANU were able to use as the basis of their policy as a government.

The lesson of all this should have been that KANU were a driving force whose electoral advantage over KADU was likely to be held or increased. Furthermore, they represented among others the Kikuyu, the most powerful group politically in the new Kenya. Against these political realities had to be set the moral debt which the British Government owed to KADU for taking up the reins of government after the 1961 elections. There was clearly a dilemma, but what should have been uppermost in British Ministers' minds was the fact that nothing they could do would, in the long term, prevent the majority (i.e. KANU) from prevailing. When this happened, KADU would inevitably feel let down. The question was, or should have been, at what stage KADU ought to be faced with the truth.

The question arose in an acute form at the constitutional conference in 1962, which began in February, lasted throughout March, came several times to the verge of break-down, and finally ended with the formation of a KANU–KADU Coalition Government in early April, eight weeks after it had begun.

Deadlock bedevilled the conference, and its cause was simple— the insistence by KADU that the structure of government that was decided for Kenya should be regional, and that the regions should have authority. Their regional plan had been elaborated and placed as a formal proposal before the conference. A compromise proposal put forward by Sir Ralph Hone, the independent constitutional adviser to the conference, which provided for a number of local government boards, was rejected out of hand by KADU. Disagreements arose in detail over the control of land, and the control of the police, but essentially the difference was the fundamental one of the type of government independent Kenya should have. In the sixth week, it seemed only too likely that the conference would have to be brought to an end in failure, the consequences of which in terms of trouble in Kenya would have been serious. Mr. Reginald Maudling (who had been Colonial Secretary since the autumn of 1961) chose this moment, when everyone was bored and frustrated with sterile argument, to put before the delegates his own proposals. After nearly two further weeks of discussions and alarms, these were accepted by both sides, and the formation of a national government of KANU and KADU, with equal status for Mr. Kenyatta and Mr. Ngala, was announced.

On the face of it, the Maudling compromise gave to KADU a large measure of what they were seeking. His outline constitution provided for a strong central government, but in addition, regional governments enjoying wide autonomous powers, the most important being control of most land (except the contentious Highlands), and the police (with certain necessary reservations). That Mr. Maudling got the delegates to sign the conference agreement was certainly a triumph of chairmanship. The agreement itself, however, was of far more dubious value. As *The Times* pointed out in an editorial (April 6, 1962):

the arguments between the KANU supporters of Mr. Jomo Kenyatta and the KADU followers of Mr. Ronald Ngala have been arguments about fundamentals, not about details and niceties of wording . . . The truism that constitutions are not worth the paper they are written on unless the right spirit pervades the people who have to work them applies with more force to Kenya than to most other countries.

KANU made no secret of their belief that only with a strong unitary government could Kenya survive, economically and administratively. It was a sound enough argument, given the weaknesses and problems of the country. Apart from any other considerations, the creation of a series of regional administrations–each requiring civil servants–in a country with little money and few trained administrators, could not make sense. This was recognized not only by KANU but by British officials. Furthermore, KANU leaders made no secret of their continuing intention to press for a unitary government, and one did not have to put too fanciful an interpretation on their words to appreciate that they fully intended to get it. Mr. Kenyatta, indeed, wrote a letter to *The Times* published on March 2, 1962, which set out clearly what his policy was. After giving figures about the tribal composition of KANU and KADU (which shewed KADU to represent nine tribes, and to have won 16 per cent of the votes at the last election, against KANU's ten tribes and 67 per cent of the votes) Mr. Kenyatta wrote:

I hope that the British public will beware of the subtle, professional public relations move, to appeal to their sentiments in support of an 'artificial' underdog. The moment democratic principles are sacrificed in a wave of emotion then we will have started on the road to the ruin of even the safeguards for the individual and minorities. You cannot suppress and frustrate a majority without serious risks. We believe too in unity if we are to face up to the challenge after independence.

In short, the relative strengths of KANU and KADU being what they were, any constitution based on KADU principles and utterly

E

rejected by KANU could be no more than a ludicrous piece of make-believe. Sooner or later, the carefully constructed edifice would be shewn to be without foundations, and it would have to be dismantled. When that happened, KADU would–justifiably–be able to claim that they had been badly misled. The time to force the facts upon them, surely, was the 1962 conference. Their re-actions would have been bitter, and there would possibly have been trouble, but Britain would have been still in control of Kenya and therefore in a position to deal with it. What is more, the time remaining before independence–the period between the 1962 con-ference and the actual introduction of the constitution evolved at it, and then the period of full internal self-government leading to independence–could have been used to train administrators, to adapt the administrative machine in readiness for independence, and to give an elected government a taste of the responsibilities of power before they were left entirely on their own.

What in fact happened was quite different. The Maudling con-stitutional framework having been projected as a workable reality had to be clothed in the appropriate legal form. For months the coalition government, an uneasy marriage of KANU and KADU, mutually suspicious and out of sympathy, wrangled in committee over the details of drafting. Commissions were appointed to de-limit the boundaries of the regions and the constituencies for the lower house of the legislature. The amount of work involved in these tasks can be judged from the length of the report of the Regional Boundaries Commission (Cmnd 1899)–113 pages.

Eleven months after the 1962 conference ended, in February and March 1963, Mr. Duncan Sandys, who had by now become Secretary of State for the Colonies as well as for Commonwealth Relations, found it necessary to spend three weeks in Kenya personally sorting out the remaining points of difference between KANU and KADU on the constitution. In a statement on March 12, 1963, in the House of Commons, Mr. Sandys said there were 'about 25' such issues, the main points of disagreement being over 'the balance of power between the Central Government and the Regional authorities'. In other words, in the fundamental issue between the two African parties, there was no improvement in the situation that had nearly caused the failure of the 1962 conference. Mr. Sandys, indeed, underlined this fact in his statement when he said, 'Unhappily, the whole of political life in Kenya today is permeated by inter-tribal rivalry and suspicion . . .' He himself had been obliged to impose decisions on the points of disagreement and in doing so, he said, he was guided by three main principles.

The first was to adhere faithfully to the basic constitutional framework agreed between all parties at the Lancaster House conference last year. The second was to create governmental machinery which would be efficient and workable. The third was to provide a sufficient degree of regional autonomy to safeguard one tribal group from domination by another.

One of his decisions was to create a seventh region (there were to have been six), consisting of the most strongly Somali part of the former Northern Frontier District (about which I shall write below).

On April 18, 1963, the mountains finally gave birth, not to a mouse, but to what was probably the most complicated colonial constitution ever produced by the British Colonial Office. It appeared only two days before nomination day for the elections fought in May. The constitution* included 233 clauses, in fourteen chapters, plus seven schedules, covering altogether 223 pages.

The May 1963 election was crucial, since it produced the government which would lead Kenya into independence. It was pretty clear that KANU would win, and in the event they won far more handsomely than most observers had predicted. Almost immediately, Mr. Tom Mboya, as Minister of Justice and Constitutional Affairs in Mr. Kenyatta's first Government, arrived in London with two colleagues to hold preliminary discussions at the Colonial Office on the constitutional amendments necessary before the internal self-government constitution became the constitution for independence. He made it quite plain that KANU intended to change the constitution. And he remarked at a press conference:

We envisage that the constitutional conference will be a conference between the British Government and the Kenya Government essentially. We shall have token representation by the opposition . . . But Kenya is going to be governed by the Kenya Government and not by the opposition.

His attitude–typical of a man who, whatever his faults, understands the realities of power–not surprisingly caused consternation

* Statutory Instrument No. 791 of 1963, *The Kenya Order in Council, 1963.*

in the ranks of KADU and of the substantial section of British Conservative M.P.s who supported KADU.

The important controversial matter at this stage was the amendment procedure which was to be incorporated in the independence constitution. (An internal self-government constitution contains no procedure for amendment, since amendment is possible only by legislative action by the colonial power. In a case like Kenya's, therefore, where the intention was for the internal self-government constitution to be essentially the constitution for independence, the only necessary changes were the removal of the Governor's reserved powers and the inclusion of amendment procedure.) When asked about this, Mr. Mboya, at the same press conference, said ominously, 'I think the position is very clear. Either you have a constitution that will work, or you don't.' If the constitution could not be changed constitutionally, people would change it unconstitutionally. The significance of his remark was that a procedure had been agreed in the pre-election constitutional talks; changes in such fundamental matters as the rights of regions could be made only by a 75 per cent majority of the lower house and a 90 per cent majority in the Senate. Even with their electoral victory, KANU could not hope to obtain such a Senate majority without KADU support.

KANU's argument now was reasonable enough. It was that effective government would not be possible under a system which imposed on Kenya an administration sophisticated well beyond her means, and further, that it was wrong that an elected government, manifestly enjoying majority support, should be hampered at every turn by the minority. Reasonable though these arguments were, they had to be set against the undoubted fact that the constitutional framework had been agreed by KANU, as well as KADU and the British Government. As I have already explained, KANU never had much intention of sticking to the agreement— but they did sign it. What is more, Lord Kilmuir, speaking as Lord Chancellor in the House of Lords on May 15, 1962, emphasized that the constitutional framework agreed at the 1962 conference was 'intended to be the constitution which Kenya will have when it attains independence'. Mr. Mboya and his colleagues, after the election, claimed to believe that the rigid amendment procedure was intended not for independence but for internal self-government.

As Kenya entered the final stage before independence, therefore, the position was as follows. It had a strong KANU Government, determined to turn upside down the constitutional safeguards incorporated at the insistence of KADU. Meanwhile, the process of transforming provinces to regions, and staffing them with adequate civil servants, was taxing the most experienced British colonial officials, and it was becoming daily more apparent that the number of Africans capable of filling the large number of posts thus created was pitifully inadequate. The British Government had been extraordinarily and culpably dilatory about giving posts of authority to Africans in time to train them on the job. Administratively, the regional system was proving to be quite unworkable, and was certain to break down, helped on its way by the KANU Government. KANU's unwillingness to compromise was probably exacerbated by the attitude of a few of the senior administrators who had still not overcome their anti-Kenyatta feelings, and were unwilling to cooperate with him.

There was one more threat to Kenya's stability that must be mentioned. It was the long-standing Somali dispute, a highly complex issue. In essence, it derived from the Somali Government's claim to the Somali-inhabited areas of Ethiopia and Kenya, and to French Somaliland, in pursuit of their ideal of 'Greater Somalia'. In Kenya, there had for years been a Somali problem, with nomadic tribesmen wandering across the national frontiers. As Kenya developed constitutionally, the problem became more acute, and a secessionist movement gained strength among the Somalis of the Northern Frontier District, who did not wish to be ruled by the Africans of Kenya.

It was to meet this wish for separation that Mr. Sandys, in March 1963, made his decision to create a seventh, Somali, region. In announcing it, he told the House of Commons, in reply to questions, that the decision did not pre-judge a final decision in the Northern Frontier District 'and does not exclude further consideration of other solutions'. By May, and the election campaign, it was perfectly obvious that the creation of the new region had solved nothing. I visited Wajir, the Beau Geste fort in the middle of the Kenya desert, at that time, when there was a total boycott of the elections and found evidence of a growing determination to secede. The Government of the Somali Republic set out its views as the Kenya election ended, in a White Paper distributed in

Nairobi and called *The Issue of the Northern Frontier District*. This called on the British Government, before independence, to 'recognize the right of the people of the N.F.D. to self-determination in accordance with their will as expressed to the Independent N.F.D. commission'. The N.F.D. commission, appointed by the British Government, had reported in December 1962 (Cmnd 1900). They had found that opinion in the eastern part of the N.F.D. was almost unanimously in favour of secession from Kenya and adherence to the Somali Republic. In his March 1963 statement, Mr. Sandys had said, 'Even if we wanted to do so, it was clear that in these circumstances a decision by the British Government to cede this territory without the consent of Kenya Ministers would have provoked violent reactions throughout the country . . .'

This was true enough. Had the British Government decided to permit secession of at least a part of the Somali area before the internal self-government period, however, Britain would have been the responsible power, and able to deal with the trouble–just as she would have been able to deal with the trouble that would have arisen had she faced KADU with the facts of power in Kenya at that stage. The British Government did not act, but in August 1963 called a conference in Rome with the Somali Government and the Kenya Government to discuss the question. By this time, clearly, it was too late to take any step opposed by the Kenya Government, who were then only four months away from the agreed date of independence. The Somali issue was left unsolved, to create for the newly independent Government of Kenya a major problem of internal security, to tackle which they have had to rely heavily on British military logistic support.

The fundamental dispute over the type of government which independent Kenya should have–strong at the centre or strong in the regions–came up finally, and with the greatest possible display of ill-will, at the final pre-independence conference in London in September and October 1963. As the parties gathered their demands were just as they had always been–KANU were determined to end the regional system and KADU, who had been further weakened since the election by members crossing the floor of the House, were determined to preserve it. The discussions had to take place between the British Government and the two parties separately, rather than in conference. A crisis arose when KADU members in Kenya threatened to partition the country, and Mr. Ngala had to send one of his lieutenants home to sort matters out. He bitterly–and with justice–accused the British Government of failing to keep an undertaking to implement the regional constitution, and pointed out that it would be no good his going after independence to the KANU Government to get them to implement it. To complicate things further, the KANU delegation, claiming that Mr. Sandys, the Colonial Secretary, was yielding to threats by KADU, themselves threatened to walk out.

In fact Mr. Sandys's position was quite different. He had to reach a decision in impossible circumstances. In the first place, the British Government was solemnly pledged to uphold the 1962 regional constitution. They were under much pressure from an influential part of the Conservative Party not to betray this pledge. At the same time, they had been bludgeoned some months earlier into fixing the date for Kenya's independence (December 12), KANU's argument having been that only by fixing a date could the East African Federation be formed. (Even at the moment when the date was fixed, the prospects for Federation were receding.) They therefore had to launch Kenya into independence with a constitution that was acceptable to the Kenya Government, even if not by the opposition, since if they did not, they would have to answer in the House of Commons to grave charges when the independent government immediately overthrew the constitution.

It was simply not possible both to uphold the pledges and satisfy the Kenya Government. Mr. Sandys decided to break the pledges. In announcing his decision at the final session of the conference on Saturday, October 19, 1963, Mr. Sandys admitted he had departed from what had previously been agreed. He said:

I know that there are some who will feel that it was wrong of me to approve any departure whatsoever from the provisions previously agreed. I fully understand their feelings. The British Government has given most earnest thought to this problem. As a result, we came to the clear conclusion that our duty was to do what was in the true interest of Kenya in the years ahead.

The changes which he had authorized provided an alternative method (a national referendum) of amending the constitutional provisions relating to regional powers. He strengthened the central control of the police, weakening that of the regions. He centralized the public service commission, instead of perpetuating his own original idea for a commission for each region.

The Colonial Office gloss on the unhappy situation was that the 1962 agreements could not be held to be as binding as agreements between sovereign independent countries.

Mr. Ngala of KADU accused Mr. Sandys at a press conference of dishonesty. He read to the press the following letter to Mr. Sandys:

We are frankly appalled at your decision to impose changes in the present constitution without the agreement of one of the two main political parties of Kenya, in concert with the Kenya Government and in complete breach of the solemn pledges and undertakings made by you and your predecessor [Mr. Maudling] in London and in Kenya during the last 18 months.

Apart from the main issue of principle involved, there are two specific matters we wish to place on record. Firstly, we condemn it as wholly misleading, even dishonest, for you to pretend that the proposed constitutional changes are not basic but are attributable to unworkability, since the present constitution has not yet been implemented, let alone tried out in practice. Secondly, we dismiss as no less misleading the suggestion that, because certain powers to be unlawfully removed from the regions are to be handed to so-called independent central commissions rather than directly to the central Government, no breach of faith is involved. For you are well aware, allegedly independent commissions in African emergent countries come under governmental control almost before the ink is dry on their charters.

Under these circumstances, we cannot possibly accept your conclusions at the end of this conference and you will have to take sole responsibility for imposing your decisions against the will and wishes of a very significant proportion of the people of Kenya, whom we have the honour here to represent.

Nor can we share the responsibility for any of the consequences for the future of Kenya that may flow from your actions. For us to react otherwise would be wholly against our own judgment and convictions and contrary both to the best interests of all Kenya and especially of those we represent, and to the only mandate we have received from them.

Hence, as you and the Kenya Government have seen fit to repudiate in fact a constitution forming the only acceptable basis of one united Kenya, we must now regard this concept as no longer valid and hence we demand the inalienable right of the peoples and tribes we represent to separate self-determination outside the shackles of arbitrary, outdated colonial national boundaries.

I have quoted this letter in full because it expresses perfectly the feeling of betrayal which KADU felt. Of course, as everyone knows, Kenya did not split up immediately after independence. Mr. Kenyatta proved to be a far better national, as distinct from party, leader than many people had expected. KADU, weakened progressively as its members followed the normal African political habit of jumping on the bandwaggon, eventually decided to dissolve and throw in its lot with KANU. Now Mr. Ngala is vice-president of KANU, having been chosen by the party with a large majority of votes in preference to the former vice-president of Kenya, Mr. Oginga Odinga, now in opposition.

In the circumstances at the time of the final conference, the British Government could have taken no other course than that which Mr. Sandys did in fact take. To insist on the retention of the 1962 constitution would have been completely irresponsible, because the Kenya Government would certainly not have respected it. But the circumstances were no different from those which had prevailed for months. There was no basic difference between the realities of power at the end of 1963 and the realities of power in March 1962. They were simply more concentrated. If the British Government, in the person of Mr. Maudling, had accepted the situation as it was in 1962, the elaborate nonsense of the 1962 constitution would never have been invented. Even a year later, when Mr. Sandys had to make his decisions on outstanding points of difference, he ought to have recognized publicly that what was being laid down was unworkable. The longer the farce was continued, the deeper the British Government became involved in commitments and obligations. No one had the courage to recognize that Mr. Maudling's triumph of chairmanship was unrealistic. No one had the courage to change a policy that was doomed to failure. Nothing was done until action could be avoided no longer, and then the decisions that had to be made, that should have been made before, were perforce dishonourable decisions.

The fact that they were realistic, the fact that Kenya since independence has done better than most observers expected, the fact that President Kenyatta has shewn a degree of statesmanship which many people find surprising, all these are irrelevant. It was not the Kenya Government's good faith that was in question at the end of 1963, but the British Government's. Its dishonourable decisions need never have been made if the policy which Mr. Macleod launched in 1960 had been properly thought through.

Chapter 6

Uganda's Lost Counties

UNLIKE Kenya, Uganda did not suffer from a white settler problem. Its main difficulty was, and still is, another conflict of peoples, namely the relationship between Buganda, the central, traditionally powerful kingdom whose leader is the Kabaka, and the rest of the country. It is complicated by the existence of other traditional areas–the kingdoms of Bunyoro, Toro and Ankole and the district of Busoga–which in some respects have been on the same side as Buganda in the conflict, but in others have been anti-Buganda. The most obvious example where the trade union of kings did not work was the dispute between Buganda and Bunyoro over the so-called lost counties (about which I shall write below). Because of the predominant educational and economic position of Buganda, however, and the fact that the Kabaka's kingdom includes both Kampala, the capital, and Entebbe, the other main town of Uganda, it is the relationship between Buganda and the rest of Uganda which has been the most important factor in the development of Uganda to independence.

By the 1960s it was not a new problem, nor an unfamiliar one. The Kabaka's government enjoyed a wide measure of internal self-government for many years, under the 1900 Uganda Agreement with the British Government. After the Second World War, a whole series of troubles and disputes began, during a period when (from 1953) the powers and responsibilities of the Kabaka's Government were being widely extended, and the matters over which they had control increased. In that year, the Lukiiko (the Buganda Parliament) called for independence from the rest of Uganda and refused to nominate Buganda representatives to the Uganda Legislative Council. A month after this action, the British Government, in the person of the Governor, Sir Andrew Cohen, held the Kabaka to be in breach of the 1900 Agreement, and deposed him, exiling him to Britain. He returned two years later in 1955 under the terms of an agreement (the Namirembe Agreement) drawn up in accordance with the advice of a commission presided over by Sir Keith Hancock. The main recommendations of the Hancock Commission were that Buganda should remain an integral part of the protectorate of Uganda, that Buganda's affairs should be conducted by ministers and the Kabaka, though his traditional dignities should be respected, should in future be a constitutional monarch, and that the Lukiiko should agree to Buganda's representation in the Legislative Council. As a pointer to future developments this was of great significance, first because it envisaged the 'democratization' of Buganda, and the reduction of the Kabaka's personal powers of rule, and secondly because it reaffirmed that Buganda, whatever its privileges, was essentially a part of Uganda as a whole.

At the same time, the reaction of Buganda to the Namirembe Agreement, was equally significant of things to come. In fact the Lukiiko refused to send Buganda representatives to the central legislature, and fought a prolonged legal battle (unsuccessfully) to justify their refusal. Their legal arguments were finally rejected in November 1960. The Lukiiko at this period once again sought the abrogation of the Buganda agreements and the end of British protection, and most Buganda voters obeyed the Lukiiko's call to boycott registration of voters for the forthcoming election, which Mr. Macleod, then Colonial Secretary, nevertheless decided should continue. The Buganda disagreement with the British Government came to a head once more at the end of 1960, when the Buganda Government called for independence to be granted to it, setting a deadline of December 31. In practice, the deadline was, needless to say, ignored by the British Government, and things continued more or less normally. The call for independence was a gesture rather than a genuine political demand. The circumstances that led to its being made were real enough, and were rightly taken seriously by the British Government. Mr. Macleod had already appointed a Uganda Relationships Commission (which began its work in January 1961) under the chairmanship of Lord Munster, to examine the relationships between the various parts of Uganda and to make recommendations.

The Munster Commission reported in June 1961. It examined fully the feelings of the Buganda Government, as exemplified in their abortive declaration of independence, but it held strongly the view that Uganda ought to remain a single state with a strong central government. Buganda should enjoy a federal relationship with the rest of the country but should definitely not be allowed to secede. Secession, the report declared, would 'remove the heart from the country'.* Lord Munster and his colleagues, in other words, had reasserted what had been British policy towards Uganda ever since the relationships question became a major point at issue. In 1953, Sir Andrew Cohen and the Kabaka (before his exile), in announcing the Buganda constitutional changes, had agreed that Buganda should continue to play its part 'as a province and component part of the protectorate'. In 1955, in the Namirembe Agreement on the return of the Kabaka to his country, the status of Buganda as a province of Uganda had been once again underlined.

Even earlier the broad principles had been laid down by a previous Governor, Sir John Hall. He in 1947 asserted not only that Uganda was to be a primarily African state—an assertion possible even at that period in a country where white settlers did not have a vested interest in keeping control in European hands—but that its form of government should not be unitary, and that there must be special provision for the traditional kingdoms.

At the same time, the Relationships Commission did not minimize the strength and depth of the feelings in Buganda, and their proposals provided for recognition of Buganda's special position. To quote the report: 'We do not think that Buganda could be asked to come into a new constitution with less independence than she already enjoys; and she could well enjoy more, so long as she plays her true part in a united Uganda.'

The facts which were the *raison d'être* of the Relationships Commission provided the background to the constitutional conference which opened in September 1961 in London, under the chairmanship of Mr. Iain Macleod – his last appearance as Colonial Secretary, for his translation to the Leadership of the House of Commons was announced on the day the Uganda conference ended.

The report of the Relationships Commission was on the table at the conference as the basic document for the constitutional discussions. When the conference opened, the question of Buganda's status was still unsettled and even before it began, it was clear that there were going to be difficulties. Indeed, until a matter of

* *Report of the Uganda Relationships Commission, 1961*, Government Printer, Uganda.

hours before the formal opening session, it was by no means certain that the Buganda delegation would attend. That they did was due partly to their own realization that if they stayed away while the future of Uganda was being decided they would be the losers in the long term, partly to the diplomacy of Mr. Macleod, working behind the scenes, and partly to the astute political skill of Dr. Milton Obote, now the President of Uganda, but then leader of the Opposition (the government being formed by the Democratic Party under Mr. Benedicto Kiwanuka). Subsequent events have shewn Dr. Obote to be a tough and expert politician. At that time, little was known about him, but it was significant that he had grasped immediately the essential point of Uganda politics–the need to keep Buganda within the national framework. His covert liaison with the Baganda had tactical overtones. Mr. Kiwanuka who is a Muganda himself, was at odds with the Kabaka and his supporters. The fact that he had fought the election, when Buganda generally was boycotting it, was one indication of this, but the dispute went far deeper than that. Dr. Obote is a member of one of Uganda's smaller tribes, and to him and his Uganda People's Congress the electoral support of the Baganda at the next election would be of crucial importance–and so it proved, when the U.P.C. routed the Democratic Party and formed a government in alliance (later broken) with the Kabaka Yekka, the Buganda 'King's Party'. Above the considerations of party tactics, however, Dr. Obote's assistance in persuading the Baganda to cooperate was of strategic importance for the future of Uganda itself. It was in fact the first occasion on which representatives from Buganda had taken part in constitutional discussions alongside representatives from the rest of the country.

After various alarums and excursions (including a walk-out by Mr. Kiwanuka) the 1961 conference agreed on a constitutional framework under which Buganda would enjoy a federal relationship with the rest of the country, having a measure of autonomy in a number of legislative matters, and also having its own courts (or rather, a separate Buganda High Court whose judges would be the same as those of the High Court of Uganda). The other kingdoms were to enjoy similar, but more constricted, autonomous rights–a semi-federal rather than a truly federal relationship as was specifically asserted in the summary of proposals issued after the 1961 conference (Cmnd 1523).

That agreement was obtained to this constitutional framework was a major achievement, and one which has had lasting effects on the development of Uganda as an independent country. Important though it was, and significant though it was of the increasing acceptance by Buganda of its position as a part of Uganda rather than as a state on its own, the 1961 agreement was not a final solution to the relationships problem. This was explicitly recognized in the conference document, which stated under the heading Internal Boundary Disputes:

(a) General. The National Assembly will have power to appoint a Commission to investigate boundary disputes and make recommendations.

(b) The Buganda/Bunyoro boundary. The Secretary of State will ask the Prime Minister [of Great Britain] to appoint a Commission of Privy Councillors to investigate this important dispute.

The Buganda/Bunyoro boundary dispute was over the so-called lost counties. It was crucial to the whole relationship of Buganda, not only with its neighbour, Bunyoro, but with the rest of Uganda, since any solution to the dispute must involve the central Government (and did in fact bring the central Government into conflict with Buganda when the issue came to settlement after independence). The British Government's attitude and action–or rather, failure to act–in the matter of the lost counties is, in my view, the essence of the shortcomings of British colonial policy towards Uganda. It is, therefore, the essence of this chapter, and must be examined in rather more detail.

The Relationships Commission had discussed the local feelings over the dispute and had recommended that a referendum should be taken in some of the lost counties to discover the wishes of the inhabitants. This proposal was unacceptable to the Buganda Government, and it was for this reason that Mr. Macleod at the 1961 conference decided on the appointment of the special Privy Councillors' commission.

Three Privy Councillors were appointed–Lord Molson as chairman, Lord Listowel and Lord Ward of Witley–in December 1961 and they visited Uganda to take evidence in January 1962, remaining the whole month in the country. Their report was ready in March, and was published in May as a White Paper (Cmnd 1717). The delay was deliberate, to avoid influencing the Uganda elections in April 1962.

The history of the dispute is complex. It was summarized in the Molson Commission's report.* Basically the trouble arose from an alliance made in 1890 between the then Kabaka and Captain (later Lord) Lugard. In 1893 the alliance was put to the test in a war against Bunyoro, as a result of which, by way of reward, Buganda was given a part of Bunyoro's territory. After a good deal of equivocation, this cession of territory was recognized officially and agreements signed by the British Government from 1900 onwards perpetuated it.

To quote the Molson Commission's report: 'It was manifest

---

* In 1869, Kabarega succeeded to the throne of Bunyoro, and in 1884 Mwanga succeeded to the throne of Buganda. These two men were to have a decisive influence on subsequent events. Kabarega was an able, aggressive king, determined to restore the fortunes of a declining Bunyoro at the expense of neighbouring tribes, including the Baganda. Unfortunately as it proved for Bunyoro, he quarrelled violently with Sir Samuel Baker in 1872, and henceforth earned a reputation of unremitting hostility to all foreign influence. Mwanga, the Kabaka of Buganda, though destined, like Kabarega, to end his days in exile, succeeded during the crucial early days in enlisting British support for his régime and for the territorial expansion of Buganda in return for his military assistance.

In 1890, Captain Lugard (later Lord Lugard), the agent of the Imperial British East Africa Company in Uganda, concluded a treaty under which Mwanga acknowledged the suzerainty of the Company in return for assurance by the Company that it would uphold his authority in Buganda.

The first clash between the British and Bunyoro came in 1891 when Lugard led an expedition to western Uganda for the purpose of recruiting Sudanese troops left there by Emin Pasha, and incidentally, with the intention of restoring to the throne of Toro, Kasagama, the young heir who had been driven into exile in Buganda by Kabarega. Eventually, after much hesitation, including a short-lived decision to withdraw British influence completely from Uganda, the moral obligation to defend Kasagama from the vengeance of Kabarega compelled Colonel Colville in December 1893 to launch a full-scale military campaign against Kabarega and the Banyoro. Kabarega suffered a series of defeats. In November 1894, he was driven from his country and forced to take refuge among the Nilotic Lango people across the Nile.

In the meantime, the British Government had declared a Protectorate over the Kingdom of Buganda by a notice published in the London Gazette on June 19, 1894. The declaration specifically excluded the territories adjoining Buganda, including Bunyoro. On June 9, 1894, Colonel Colville was instructed by the Foreign Office to confine his military operations and occupation of forts in Bunyoro to measures which might be necessary to secure the defence of Buganda, and 'that any temporary and partial occupation of Unyoro must be for purely defensive purposes'.

from the earliest days of the century that the Banyoro refused to be reconciled to the loss of territory ceded to Buganda.' There were several petitions claiming the return of the counties to Bunyoro but to all (again quoting the commission) 'the reply invariably was that the Secretary of State could not alter a decision which had been reaffirmed on many occasions and that the boundaries laid down in the 1900 Agreement could not be changed in favour of Bunyoro'.

This long and acrimonious dispute between Buganda and Bunyoro in which the British Government in effect supported Buganda, was the background against which the Relationships Commission had worked, and had made their recommendation of a referendum. In looking at it, the Molson Commission took into account recent developments in Buganda (the series of disputes with the British Government on status and relationship to the rest of Uganda) and constitutional developments for Uganda itself. They examined in careful detail every aspect of the situation, from topography to security, and they examined charges of discrimination levelled by Bunyoro against the Kabaka's Government. At

---

Without, apparently, any prior consultation with the British Government, Colonel Colville promised the Buganda chiefs in the early part of 1894 that all Bunyoro territory south of the Kafu river would be incorporated in Buganda, and divided equally between the Protestant and Catholic chiefs. Colonel Colville was forced by illness to leave Uganda suddenly, and this promise did not become known to Mr. E. J. L. Berkeley who succeeded him until December 1895. As part of the process of rehabilitating Bunyoro, which had been devastated by the campaign against Kabarega, Berkeley had previously agreed that a Munyoro chief, Rabadongo, should be put in charge of 'south-east Unyoro'. This was roughly the area now comprising the present sazas of Buyaga and Bugangazzi in Buganda. When told of Colville's promise by the Buganda chiefs and the Catholic bishop of Buganda, Berkeley with the consent of the Foreign Office countermanded his arrangements and, in accordance with Colville's undertaking, confirmed the incorporation in Buganda of all territory south of the Kafu river. Two British officers serving in Bunyoro at this time, Pulteney and Foster, resigned their posts in protest against this decision.

On April 13, 1896, the British Protectorate was formally extended to Bunyoro and the other territories adjoining Buganda.

In 1900 the British Commissioner in Uganda, Sir Harry Johnston, signed on behalf of the British Government a comprehensive agreement with the Kabaka, chiefs and people of Buganda in amplification of the previous agreement signed by Colville in 1894.

the end of their survey, they took a grave view of the situation and wrote in their report of

increasing hostility between the Kabaka's Government and the leaders of the Banyoro. There has been no sign of reconciliation between the antagonists; on the contrary, it was apparent that with the passage of time relations have become steadily worse. The prospect of the termination of the British Protectorate makes the Banyoro feel that an impartial arbiter will be withdrawn. The increased autonomy which Buganda will enjoy under the 1961 constitution adds greatly to the apprehensions of the Banyoro.

Even more gloomily, they added:

We must state plainly that if the appointment of our Commission does not improve matters, it will make them far worse. Our appointment was almost the first recognition by Her Majesty's Government that the Banyoro have a case and that it should be impartially examined. Our report finds that a substantial part of the Banyoro claim is justified. If these claims are not met in the near future, obviously the situation will be far more dangerous than in the past.

The solution which Lord Molson and his colleagues proposed was a compromise intended to produce a solution, as they declared, 'on broad lines of equity'. They advocated a limited transfer of territory. Of the five counties, and two parts of counties, in dispute, two counties should be returned to Bunyoro, the rest should remain in Buganda (but Mubende Town, a place of particular significance for the Banyoro, though in the Buganda part, should be added to the list of Uganda towns to be administered directly by the central government).

After pointing out the difficulties likely to be placed by Buganda in the way of a solution on these lines, the Molson Commission added:

The major political parties have expressed the wish that this dispute should be settled by the British Government before independence. They have both suggested that this is a moral duty which Her Majesty's Government should discharge before withdrawing from the country. With this view we agree because it is certain that the tranquillity and perhaps the stability of the newly-independent state would be imperilled if the dispute continued . . . If all the measures for obtaining agreement which we have suggested should unfortunately fail, then the people of the Protectorate will expect Her Majesty's Government to take such

F

steps as are necessary to settle this problem before independence and in accordance with our recommendations.

In view of the subsequent behaviour of the British Government, it is worth looking at the terms of reference of the Commission. They were as follows:

Having regard to the paramount need for the people of Uganda including Buganda to move together into independence in conditions which will ensure them peace and contentment, to investigate allegations of discrimination of the kind contained in the Omukama of Bunyoro's petition and grievances referred to in the Munster Report concerning areas in Buganda which are named below, to receive representations from those concerned and to advise whether any, *and if so what*, measures should be taken to deal with the situation . . . [my italics].

In the next paragraph of their report (which was to Mr. Macmillan, the Prime Minister) the commission added, 'In a letter to our chairman you confirmed, what was in fact already clear, that these terms of reference left us free to recommend any solution we thought appropriate, including a transfer of territory.' This letter from Mr. Macmillan was later described by the Kabaka's Government–which apparently did not know of it at the time when the terms of reference were being discussed–as a 'significant factor concealed'.

There are several points worth underlining. In the first place, the British Government, after years–more than half a century–of refusal to alter the *de facto* position of the lost counties, in spite of many requests from Bunyoro, decided at the September 1961 constitutional conference that the issue needed to be settled. The appointment of a commission of Privy Councillors was an unusual step which would hardly have been taken if it had not been thought necessary, since the mere fact of appointing the commission must suggest to all interested parties that the lost counties question was still unsettled. Secondly, the terms of reference of Lord Molson's commission, including as they did the injunction to suggest any course of action that might be necessary, reinforced the impression that action was contemplated. It would, after all, have been pointless to ask the Privy Councillors to propose a solution if there was no intention of accepting their proposal, since that would simply exacerbate the discontent of one party or the other–or even both. It is arguable (and in 1962 it was being argued in some quarters) that the lost counties dispute had been unnecessarily revived by the Munster Commission's report. Whether that is correct, or whether the dispute was rekindled by the rapid approach of independence, is beside the point. In 1961 the British Government had accepted that it was a real dispute to which a solution had still to be found. In proposing a solution, the Molson Commission as we have seen emphasized the gravity of the problem and the likely repercussions of failure to act.

At the September 1961 conference Uganda received not only the outline of its independence constitution, duly agreed by the country's political representatives. It received also a tentative independence date–October 9, 1962 (the date on which independence actually came). Certain constitutional details still remained to be discussed, and for that reason another conference was arranged. It took place in June 1962. When it opened on June 12, it was clear that it would have to do rather more than tie up a few loose ends left from the 1961 conference. Its main task would be to try once more to find a solution to the Buganda relationships question, against the background of the Molson Commission's recommendations on the lost counties.

What is more, the political balance within Uganda had changed completely since the previous conference. Mr. Kiwanuka's Democratic Party had been defeated in the April election; Mr. Kiwanuka himself lost his seat. Dr. Obote was Prime Minister, and his Uganda People's Congress, a radical party, relied on the support of the ultra-conservative Kabaka Yekka. Dr. Obote, not himself a Muganda, had to tread delicately round any difficulty, such as the lost counties dispute, which threatened the status of Buganda. Dr. Obote's position, therefore, was unenviable, especially as he would soon be leading an independent government without even the nominal ultimate authority of Britain behind him.

This was the state of affairs when Mr. Maudling, the Colonial Secretary, opened the conference in Marlborough House. Both he and Dr. Obote, in their public speeches on this occasion, avoided direct references to the lost counties question, though outside the conference room, in an interview with me, Dr. Obote had argued that it was a security matter, not a constitutional issue, and that the British Government would be doing Uganda a dis-service if they insisted on achieving a settlement before independence. Dr. Obote denied that his attitude was influenced by his alliance with the Kabaka Yekka, though in view of Buganda's reaction to the Molson Report, he would hardly have strengthened the alliance by admitting that a settlement on the Molson lines was even remotely desirable. Two weeks after the publication of the Molson Report, on May 18, the Kabaka's Government had published their own paper entitled *Buganda's Position, II: Lord Molson is Wrong*, firmly and furiously rejecting both what had been proposed and the commission's right to propose it. It was in this document that they commented on the concealment from the Kabaka of Mr. Macmillan's letter of amplification of the terms of reference of the Molson Commission.

The British Government's position was clear. Having agreed both the principle and the date of independence for Uganda, they, through Mr. Maudling, had to ensure as well as they could that the country should enter independence as free as possible of any circumstances likely to create or increase instability. That was not, of course, a responsibility peculiar to Uganda. It is the basic duty of a colonial power which is about to hand over authority to those whom it has hitherto been governing.

As we have seen in the case of the Somali dispute with Kenya over the former Northern Frontier District, there comes a time, when a colony is on the eve of independence, when it is difficult, or even impossible, for the colonial power to exercise in practice the powers which it still possesses legally, when by doing so it would be acting against the wishes of the elected government. This was the excuse for doing nothing, in 1963, about the Somali issue, and at that stage, it was a valid excuse. It was the excuse produced in 1962 by Mr. Maudling for failing to act on the recommendations of the Molson Commission with regard to the lost counties. Explaining his view at a press conference, Mr. Maudling said that in a situation in which the wishes of Bunyoro and of Buganda were absolutely irreconcilable no solution could be found which would be acceptable to all. With the truth of such a glimpse of the obvious few could quarrel. With its validity as an argument for abdicating responsibility it is much easier to take issue.

On June 27, 1962 Mr. Maudling announced to the Uganda conference his ruling on the lost counties question. He decided first that there was to be no immediate transfer of territory.

Secondly, the claim by Bunyoro to the four counties which the Molson commission recommended should remain under Buganda rule would lapse. For the other two counties, the National Assembly of Uganda (the central Parliament), not less than two years after the conference, would fix a date for the holding of a referendum. In this referendum the inhabitants would have three choices. They could decide to remain under the rule of Buganda; they could choose to be transferred to Bunyoro; or they could decide to remain permanently under the direct rule of the central Government of Uganda.

On behalf of his government, Dr. Obote accepted the responsibility thus placed upon him. This included the administration by the centre of the two disputed counties in the interim period, which would be likely to (and in fact did) provoke ill-will and obstruction from Buganda. As Mr. Maudling frankly recognized, one weakness of his scheme was that after independence Britain would no longer have any means of enforcing it. The Uganda National Assembly could if it wished postpone indefinitely the holding of the referendum. It also seemed clear at the time that, depending as he did on the parliamentary support of Buganda, Dr. Obote might be persuaded not to make a reality of central control over the two counties, but leave them under the *de facto* control of Buganda.

I should remark at this stage that these developments did not occur. Dr. Obote carried out the responsibilities which he had accepted. He held the referendum, in 1964, in spite of the strenuous opposition of Buganda. (The coalition broke up, Dr. Obote having by this time won greater parliamentary strength mainly through the alliance of the Democratic Party members who crossed the floor of the assembly.)

In my chapter on Ghana I wrote that the fact that things had gone wrong after independence could not be blamed on the colonial power, provided that all reasonable steps had been taken to prepare the newly independent country for its new status. The converse of this is also true. If a country is left with unsolved problems by the colonial power – problems that that power ought properly to have solved – it cannot be said that the responsibilities of colonialism have been adequately fulfilled. The new country has not been properly prepared for independence. On the contrary, its new and necessarily inexperienced government has to tackle in addition to the normal hazards of statecraft some that should already have been removed. It may be that in spite of these additional burdens, in spite of this partial failure by the colonial power to prepare the colony for independence, the potential dangers and difficulties do not materialize. This has been true of Uganda. It does not, however, alter the failure to meet responsibility. Just as the fact that things went badly wrong cannot be blamed on Britain in the case of Ghana, the fact that fission did not take place in Uganda does not absolve the British Government of 1962 from blame for its irresponsibility. The Cabinet's decision to allow Mr. Maudling to ignore the solemn recommendations of a commission appointed by the British Prime Minister specifically to make recommendations, was an act of cynical irresponsibility, a gamble that came off but ought never to have been made.

That no more serious repercussions arose is due almost entirely to the skill of Dr. Obote, who after independence had to balance precariously on the tightrope of Uganda politics, gradually strengthening the party system, and his own party, until he was in a position to assert the authority of the elected government over the traditional prestige of the kingdoms (including, indeed especially, Buganda). In June 1963, less than a year after Uganda became independent, I was visiting the country and was able to see something of Dr. Obote's ability to keep the temperature down. At that time, his Government's efforts to administer the two lost counties from the centre had been severely hampered by the presence in the disputed area of the Kabaka himself, on an extended 'hunting trip'.

A year later, in 1964, Dr. Obote's Government had put before Parliament a Bill providing for a referendum in the lost counties in November 1964 (in which the vote went overwhelmingly in favour of Bunyoro). He had, in other words, carried out to the letter the responsibilities placed on his shoulders at the 1962 London conference. In August 1964, as the referendum Bill was being discussed, the coalition between the Uganda People's Congress and the Kabaka Yekka broke up when the Kabaka Yekka members left the Government benches. In purely political terms, this was the penultimate step in the steady progress which Dr. Obote had been making, since before independence, to strengthen his own parliamentary position and his own support in the country. He had used the period of his alliance with the Kabaka Yekka to whittle away the strength of the Democratic Party. By April 1964 he had achieved for the U.P.C. on its own an overall majority in the House. When the alliance actually broke up–Buganda having failed to exercise a veto over the decision to hold the lost counties referendum–the parliamentary leader of the Democratic Party, Mr. Basil Bataringaya, crossed the floor to join forces with the U.P.C., which by this time could justly claim to be a truly national party. In addition, the Kabaka of Buganda had been elected Head of State–a King holding the office of President in a country which does not describe itself as a republic. In Uganda, the presidency was a ceremonial office and the President a constitutional rather than an executive head of state, political power resting in the Prime Minister's hands. This was a position which many observers thought the Kabaka and his followers would not accept. The lost counties referendum issue proved finally that he had no choice.

In the two years from independence Milton Obote, who at the 1961 constitutional conference had been almost an unknown figure, had achieved what successive British régimes had failed to achieve, or had believed to be not worth even trying. He had established the authority of the centre over Buganda in the most contentious of the controversial matters between them.

Since then, early in 1966, Dr. Obote has had more trouble, and in February 1966 decided to imprison some of his ministers and suspend the constitution. At the time of writing it is not clear precisely what is behind these difficulties. What is clear, however, is that Dr. Obote's assertion of central authority over Buganda in the immediate post-independence period was a personal triumph for him and a tribute to his skill as a politician. The British Government should not have allowed things to get to the point where it was necessary for him to win his triumph.

Chapter 7

Northern Rhodesian Uncertainties

As an example of the worst aspects of British colonial policy, the case of Northern Rhodesia (now Zambia) must rank high. Throughout 1961, and well into 1962, the battle over the constitutional progress of Northern Rhodesia raged furiously between the British and Federal Rhodesian Governments. Negotiations went on continually, and often acrimoniously. Decisions were made and unmade. Pressures were brought to bear, threats were uttered, tempers flared. The British Government staggered through it all, battered on all sides, conducting matters of high policy in a hole and corner fashion, speaking, through different ministries, with different voices. Mr. Iain Macleod, Colonial Secretary until September 1961, has written* that the Northern Rhodesia constitution of 1961, though 'more heavily criticized than all the other plans for African countries put together' was nevertheless the one with which he was most satisfied. In so far as the constitution that eventually emerged in 1962 succeeded in launching Northern Rhodesia on its final stage to independence, there may be some cause for satisfaction. But as a journalist closely observing the various stages of the struggle over a period of twelve months, I found the affair a depressing and disillusioning example of governmental drift, and of lack of courage in sticking to a policy. It was quite obvious at times that the Cabinet could not truly be said to have worked out a proper policy at all.

The reason is easy to see. What happened in Northern Rhodesia was crucial to the future of the Rhodesia and Nyasaland Federation. The decisions which the British Government were taking were therefore unpopular with the Federal Government, and federal displeasure expressed itself through the strong words of Sir Roy Welensky. His frequent blasts of invective (supported

* *Weekend Telegraph* March 12, 1965.

84

by his friends on the Conservative right wing) seemed unfailingly to turn the collective backbone of the British Cabinet to jelly, and *ad hoc* steps would be taken to mollify him. Eventually, as everyone knows, Sir Roy had to be faced, and the Federation disbanded, in conditions ensuring maximum ill-will on all sides. By then, Northern Rhodesia was already well on the way to becoming Zambia, but in the key period of constitutional development for Northern Rhodesia, the Federation was still there, kept alive by artificial respiration, but still able to kick, and still a major element in purely Northern Rhodesian affairs.

The immediate background to the events of 1961 and 1962 was the abortive Federal review conference which began at the end of 1960 (and was never continued). It achieved nothing, but underlined the fervent desire of the Africans, and particularly the African leaders of Northern Rhodesia and Nyasaland, to get out of the Federation altogether.

In February 1961, ostensibly as one of a set of territorial discussions intended to pave the way for further federal talks, the Northern Rhodesia constitutional conference resumed in London, under the chairmanship of Mr. Macleod (having been opened formally, and adjourned, in December). By the end of January it had become clear (unofficially but authoritatively) that Mr. Macleod's aim was to produce a constitution that would ensure a majority of African elected members of the legislature, though probably in voting terms nominated members and officials would still be able to weigh the scales against them. As was to be expected, the Africans (two parties, Mr. Kenneth Kaunda's United National Independence Party–UNIP–and Mr. Harry Nkumbula's African National Congress–ANC) were demanding 'one man one vote'. In practice, however, there was no doubt that they would accept something less than this as a compromise, and in February Mr. Kaunda and some of his UNIP colleagues were told that Mr. Macleod had in mind that there should be an elected (African) majority of about four or five.

The two European-dominated parties in Northern Rhodesia were the United Federal Party and the Dominion Party, of which the UFP was the more important. A branch of the federal UFP, it formed the non-official element of the government of Northern Rhodesia.

Just before the conference was due to begin, it was announced that the UFP and Dominion Party delegations were delaying their departure from Rhodesia, pending discussions on 'certain matters regarding the basis on which the conference is to be reconvened'. Meanwhile, Mr. John Roberts, nominal leader of the UFP in Northern Rhodesia, but in practice, at that time, largely dependent on instructions from Sir Roy Welensky in Salisbury, flew to London for talks with Mr. Macleod. His arrival, and the secrecy surrounding his movements, naturally created an air of foreboding among the other delegates. Apart from the African parties, these included representatives of the Liberal Party, led by Sir John Moffat, and of the chiefs.

Mr. Macleod began the work of the conference in the absence of the UFP delegation. While he did so, the Federal Government's special representative in London, Mr. Julian Greenfield, the Minister of Law, who had flown over separately, began a series of talks with the Commonwealth Relations Office (Mr. Duncan Sandys, the Secretary of State, was at this time in Salisbury, conducting a conference on Southern Rhodesia's constitution). Ostensibly these were to enable the Federal Government to keep in touch with developments in the Northern Rhodesian constitutional discussions, since the Federal Government had the right to be consulted about them. Britain's obligation to consult the Federal Government was accepted when the Federation was set up. The British Government's direct responsibility for constitutional advance in Northern Rhodesia and Nyasaland was reaffirmed with the proviso that 'Her Majesty's Ministers [in the United Kingdom] would naturally seek the views of the Federal Government before advising Her Majesty'. Subsequently the obligation was referred to in the House of Commons by Mr. Macmillan. This right to be consulted was time and again a bone of contention between the British and Federal Governments, the Federal Government demanding in practice that consultation should be interpreted to mean approval by Salisbury of decisions made by Whitehall. This was always hotly denied, and the British Government always maintained that they were not yielding to federal pressure, though the actual practice of consultation made this difficult to accept.

In the case of Northern Rhodesia (and Nyasaland), the division of responsibility between Federal and British Governments was, or should have been, clear. It was set out unequivocally in the preamble to the Federal constitution which stated that the two northern protectorates should continue

under the special protection of Her Majesty, to enjoy separate governments for so long as their respective peoples so desire, those governments remaining responsible (subject to the ultimate authority of Her Majesty's Government in the United Kingdom) for, in particular, the control of land in those territories, and for the local and territorial political advancement of the peoples thereof.

In the all-important matter of political advancement, therefore, the Federal Government had no responsibilities and no rights beyond that of being consulted (that is, in the last analysis, told what the British Government had decided). That this was in fact the position, however much it might be questioned and challenged in Salisbury, ultimately became clear when the British Government permitted both Nyasaland and Northern Rhodesia to secede from the Federation, and gave them constitutions disapproved of by the Federal Government. Unfortunately, the British Government proved unwilling for years to assert its rights and responsibilities, allowing itself to be stampeded by the Federal Government in matters purely its own concern.

One of the most obvious examples of this unwillingness was the decision to permit Mr. Greenfield to conduct what amounted to parallel discussions on the Northern Rhodesia constitution with the Commonwealth Relations Office while Mr. Macleod was talking with the Northern Rhodesia delegates. To put it no more strongly, this was unwise. The UFP had a right to be present at the Northern Rhodesia talks—and had they exercised it, could have put across what were in effect Sir Roy Welensky's views quite properly and constitutionally. Their absence from the talks was their own affair (and was incidentally, in the long-term view, one of the most stupid blunders which Sir Roy Welensky made in his dealings with the British Government). When they had decided not to attend, the British Government should certainly have refused to have any dealings with Mr. Greenfield on the Northern Rhodesia talks. Northern Rhodesia's constitutional progress, at this stage of negotiations, was a matter for Mr. Macleod and the Northern Rhodesian delegates. The conference was, like all colonial constitutional conferences, advisory, the ultimate decision remaining with the British Parliament, but until it had worked out its advice, there was nothing on which the Federal Government should properly have been consulted, certainly nothing which warranted daily talks between a Federal minister and the Commonwealth Secretary (or his deputy) who, though responsible for relations with the Federation, had no responsibility for Northern Rhodesia's internal affairs.

During the weekend of February 4 to 6, 1961, Mr. Greenfield, and Mr. A. D. Evans (later Sir Atholl Evans), a senior Federal civil servant, were guests at Chequers of Mr. Macmillan, the Prime Minister. Efforts were made to depict this visit as a normal courtesy extended to a senior visiting minister from a Commonwealth country, and the guest list was carefully arranged so as to emphasize the fact that the British–Federal talks were separate from the Northern Rhodesian conference. Whatever might be asserted in Whitehall, however, it was perfectly obvious to any journalist covering the situation – and even more to the delegates at the conference – that Northern Rhodesia's affairs were being discussed far more pertinently outside the conference hall than within it, and that the UFP which had boycotted the conference was getting its views across by back door diplomacy.

It was moreover clear to those of us regularly covering the conference from all sources (in practice four or five journalists) that the view of the situation taken by Mr. Macleod was very different from that of Mr. Sandys, who had meanwhile returned from his Southern Rhodesia negotiations in Salisbury. Mr. Macleod's aim, as I have explained, was an African majority of elected members. Mr. Greenfield, who as a negotiator was a master of nearly incomprehensible minutiae, had been working hard in his talks with Mr. Sandys and his colleagues, all his efforts being directed to the retention of power in what the Federal Government liked to call 'civilized and responsible hands'. This meant in fact 'white hands'. It cannot be over-emphasized that the Federal philosophy of partnership was a variant of a policy of white domination. It reached its zenith after the break-up of the Federation in the policies of the successive governments of Southern Rhodesia, all mediocre in ability, each more reactionary and repressive than its predecessor.

Lord Malvern, the first Federal Prime Minister, is famous for his remark about partnership between whites and blacks being the partnership of horse and rider, but his view was not unusual.

In speech after speech, Federal ministers made it clear that any African politician disagreeing with UFP policies was a 'self-appointed trouble-maker, unrepresentative of the mass of Africans'. I think it important to emphasize this, because much of the pressure put on the British Government by its own back-benchers and supporters in the Lords was inspired by a blind willingness to accept Sir Roy Welensky's interpretations of the situation as impartial (if not by a belief that it was right in principle to leave political control in the hands of a minority—and a racial minority at that). Let us be clear that whatever it might be called, UFP policy would have meant in practice the acceptance, not the rejection, of racialism.

As we journalists systematically went between high-level spokesmen of the Colonial Office, Commonwealth Relations Office, Federal Government and Northern Rhodesian parties, it became increasingly clear that a battle royal was going on, and that Mr. Macleod's views were by no means certain of support within the Cabinet. Not surprisingly, the Northern Rhodesian conference itself made little progress, and the participants became more and more disillusioned. Mr. Kaunda, a mild and well-balanced man, under enormous pressures from his more militant supporters both in London and at home, made a major tactical error on Thursday, February 9, 1961, when he issued a statement to the effect that the British Government should embark on a bold programme, first by granting the Africans a clear majority in both the Legislative Council and the Executive Council (the government), adding:

Secondly, the British Government should make it clear at once to Welensky and his henchman [i.e. Greenfield] that they simply must accept this if they want to avoid an uprising in Northern Rhodesia which by contrast would make Mau Mau a child's picnic. We are sincere when we say we want to avoid this, but the British Government must help us.

This was a foolish statement, as Mr. Kaunda himself quickly realized, and it was seized upon, by those looking for argument against African rule, as a threat, rather than an excitable warning. It was easy to see why it was made, however. The British Government's behaviour over the constitutional talks was hardly such as to inspire much belief in their good faith, and indeed on February 10 Mr. Kaunda, Mr. Nkumbula and Sir John Moffat went in a deputation to Mr. Macmillan and Mr. Macleod demanding, jointly, an African elected majority in the Legislative and Executive Councils.

The atmosphere, both in London and in Northern Rhodesia itself, was bad, and there were fears of serious trouble. Sir Roy Welensky alerted Federal troops – a move which the African leaders argued was an aggravation of the situation, and a proof of Federal interference in Northern Rhodesia's affairs. The security dangers were discussed also at a meeting of British Ministers. Meanwhile the conference ended, without agreement.

The all-important question of franchise qualifications had been left undecided. All that *had* been decided was that there should be a three-tier legislature, with some members chosen by an upper roll of voters, some by a lower roll. The third group would be chosen by both rolls – and each member must obtain a measure of support from both rolls as a qualification for election.

To make matters worse, on the same day on which the Northern Rhodesia conference had its final meeting (Friday, February 17) there came from Salisbury news that Mr. Joshua Nkomo, leader of the African nationalist party there (which was at that time called the National Democratic Party) had repudiated the recently achieved Southern Rhodesia constitutional agreement. He insisted that he had never accepted it, but in fact he certainly was a party to the talks and what emerged from them. He changed his mind under pressure from more militant supporters. Whatever the reason for his decision, it obviously changed entirely the circumstances of constitutional change in Southern Rhodesia, and incidentally laid the fuse of a crisis which has continued to erupt ever more seriously. It also heightened the difficulties facing the British Government over Northern Rhodesia.

What followed in the next twelve months, and particularly in the next six months, was one of the most bitterly contested constitutional wrangles that the Colonial Office had known. It is therefore worth considering what the state of affairs was, in essence, when the February conference ended. In the first place Mr. Macleod's original intention, in which he must presumably have had the support of his Cabinet colleagues, since in negotiations of this kind no Secretary of State is an entirely independent agent, had had to be amended. He had not succeeded in producing a constitutional framework under which Africans would get a small majority of elected members in the legislature. He had failed in this because the British Government had proved unable or unwilling to withstand persistent and strenuous objections, arguments and various forms of pressure imposed by the Federal Government. At the same time, the ultimate objectives had not been changed. In the White Paper in which were set out the results of the February conference (Cmnd 1295), Mr. Macleod had asserted certain principles. They included the following:

It seems to me essential that the next stage of constitutional advance should provide for a substantial increase in the number of Africans in the legislature. I myself consider that this should be achieved . . . by means which would maintain development of a non-racial approach towards politics.

His choice of the word non-racial in preference to multi-racial was deliberate and he explained that he disliked the term multi-racial. For him, non-racialism meant that those in elective office 'are there for their personal qualities rather than on account of their colour; and that the electorate is encouraged and given full opportunity to choose men who will follow policies which are in the broad national interest, rather than that of any one race alone'.

Taking into account what Federal policies meant in practice, rather than what their apologists claimed in theory, this statement implied a rejection of UFP doctrine. In view of Mr. Macleod's whole approach to the constitutional affairs of central Africa, this is not surprising, and it must further be assumed that the implications were seen and understood by his cabinet colleagues, though whether they all accepted them is another matter. They were certainly appreciated by the Federal Government and the UFP, and their reaction was to withdraw UFP members from the Executive Council of Northern Rhodesia—that is, from the government of the territory. Into the gap stepped Sir John Moffat and colleagues from the Liberal Party—thus, incidentally, performing probably their most useful service to Northern Rhodesia by providing a transition between the old colonial-federal system and the new African rule, before they themselves disappeared totally from the political scene in the 1962 election. The UFP's withdrawal, like their boycott of the conference, proved in the long term to be a major error of judgment. Even in the short term, their decision and the fierce opposition of Sir Roy Welensky to the February

White Paper gradually convinced Mr. Kaunda and Mr. Nkumbula
that from the complications of the Macleod formula they would be
likely to draw more advantage than the UFP.

The snag, which all concerned fully recognized and none more
than Mr. Macleod, was that the February White Paper framework
left many important matters undecided. The franchise details,
for example, the delimitation of constituencies, and the precise
method of election of 'national' members (that is, those in the
middle group), were to be considered by the Governor of Northern
Rhodesia in consultation with political groups. Without going into
detail, it is necessary to point out that the White Paper, discussing
the proposal for national seats, laid down in outline that candidates
for them must obtain the same minimum percentage of the votes
cast on each roll. Since the lower roll would be predominantly
African and the upper roll predominantly European, this would
mean that candidates must appeal to members of both races. This
question of the minimum percentage became in the months ahead
a subject of the bitterest and the most tendentious argument.

It soon became clear that the Federal Government did not
intend to accept the Macleod proposals, and the series of intense
diplomatic manœuvres that now began were made the more un-
friendly by the strong personal dislike that had grown up between
Sir Roy Welensky and Mr. Macleod. Many of Sir Roy Welensky's
supporters and admirers in the Conservative party in Britain
shared this dislike of a man whom Lord Salisbury–the epitome
of policies of which Mr. Macleod represented the rejection–described in the notorious phrase 'too clever by half'. In the battle
over Northern Rhodesia's constitution, this unpopularity of
Macleod certainly helped to encourage a revolt of about a hundred
Conservatives which was instrumental in persuading his Cabinet
colleagues to change their minds in June about the constitutional
framework they had accepted in February.

The Federal Government's manœuvres, conducted largely by
Mr. Greenfield, who was at this time virtually a permanent resi-
dent in London, took place in the context of far-reaching changes
in southern and central Africa. For one thing, Dr. Banda was
preparing to win handsomely the elections under the new constitution in Nyasaland–and was so confident of success that he
announced in London that he did not need to do any electioneer-
ing. Secondly, in March 1961 there took place in London the

tenth meeting since the war of Commonwealth Prime Ministers, a meeting attended by South Africa and devoted in large part to discussions which effectively expelled South Africa from the Commonwealth because of her racial policies. Sir Roy Welensky attended the meeting under the traditional arrangement which brought the Federal Prime Minister around the Commonwealth table, although his country was not independent. Far more important for him than the meeting itself, however, were the 'consultations' that went on on the fringe. He himself realized how crucial were the Federal Government's efforts to get the British Government to accept one of the federal variations on the White Paper theme of a middle group of 'National' seats – efforts which could succeed only to the extent that the British Government were ready to move away from the February decisions.

Sir Roy remarked that whether he won would depend on whether the fight was under the rules of boxing or of bridge (he is a former prize-fighter; Mr. Macleod is an expert bridge player). In the event, the rules, until June at least, were those of the boxing ring.

Mr. Greenfield and his assistants meanwhile produced slide rule interpretations of the implications in terms of representatives in the legislature of the February White Paper proposals. They argued cogently and skilfully about the delimitation of constituencies, the franchise qualifications and the system of voting by which an appeal to both races could be assured. Sir Roy put up Federal Government alternative plans for the Colonial Office to consider. UNIP, through a London representative, called on the British Government to cease negotiating with Sir Roy. Sir Roy himself left London in March, announcing that he was 'more convinced than ever' that the Federation would continue.

Discussions continued, many of them not openly admitted. Mr. Sandys, for example, travelled to Salisbury ostensibly to talks about final plans for the Southern Rhodesian constitutional White Paper. For these talks he would certainly not have needed to go to Salisbury, particularly as Sir Edgar Whitehead, then Southern Rhodesian Prime Minister, offered to come to London. The real purpose of Mr. Sandys' visit was to discuss with Sir Roy Welensky the constitution of Northern Rhodesia, about whose details the Governor of Northern Rhodesia, Sir Evelyn Hone, had been conducting talks with the various political groups in the territory.

Why was the British Government so anxious not simply to consult Sir Roy and his federal colleagues, but to try and ensure that the final decision on Northern Rhodesia was pleasing to them? The reason was that the British Government, in the first six months of 1961, were not prepared to accept the implications for the Rhodesia and Nyasaland Federation of the policy they had all but accepted for Northern Rhodesia – and that which they had fully accepted in Nyasaland.

As I have explained in an earlier chapter, the constitution given to Nyasaland in 1960 brought that country under African rule, and this meant that Nyasaland's government would inevitably be strongly opposed to continuing in the Federation. The anti-Federation views of Northern Rhodesia's African political parties were as strong as those of Nyasaland. So, for that matter, were those of Sir John Moffat's Liberals, who had become progressively more disillusioned with Federation in practice, until now they were totally opposed to it. Obviously, any constitution which brought power within reach of the African parties must at the same time cut away the foundations of the Federation. (It was also true, incidentally, that a move to the right in Southern Rhodesia, which would be encouraged by giving increased power to Africans, and which in fact took place when Sir Edgar Whitehead was defeated by the Rhodesian Front in the December 1962 elections, would also hasten the demise of the Federation. The Southern Rhodesian right-wing parties – the Dominion Party and later the Rhodesian Front of Mr. Winston Field and Mr. Ian Smith – were opposed to Federation). In dealing with constitutional developments in Northern Rhodesia the Colonial Secretary had to take into account the growing strength and importance of political awareness among the Africans, and the effect on African political views of developments elsewhere in Africa. Everything pointed to the inevitability of radical and quite rapid change to African rule. Opposition to the Federation was an important facet of the situation, though not the only one. It reflected, however, the need to meet certain criteria in Northern Rhodesia (and Nyasaland) whether or not they were acceptable to the Federal authorities.

As Colonial Secretary, Mr. Macleod certainly accepted this reading of the situation and so, it must be assumed, did the Cabinet as a whole. It was, after all, in tune with the policies of the Conservative Government since its return to power in 1959.

In his original approach to the February 1961 talks on Northern Rhodesia Mr. Macleod had been able to work along this basic line of approach. Even the February proposals, though conceived amid storms of dissension and mistrust, could be interpreted as following the general policy. Sir Roy Welensky certainly put this interpretation on them, and he recognized also that to accept them would mean accepting the likelihood of break-up for the Federation as it was, and as he wanted it to be. This was why he and his colleagues fought so bitterly and so strenuously to obtain changes in the February proposals. They were fighting not for a political gain in Northern Rhodesia, but for the very existence of the Rhodesian Federation.

As this was recognized by Sir Roy, so it was as clearly apparent to Mr. Macmillan and his colleagues. Put in simple terms, their policy for Northern Rhodesia could not fail to produce a conflict with the Federal Government. More than that, the logical outcome of what they were proposing in Northern Rhodesia was the end of the Federation in anything like its existing form. The inevitability of this conflict cannot have taken them by surprise. The opinions and attitudes of all concerned were by then known perfectly well. Nor should Mr. Macmillan have been taken unawares by reactions within his own party. The views of those Conservatives who disagreed with 'Macleod's policies' were well known, as was the fact that Sir Roy Welensky enjoyed the support of a substantial group of Conservative M.P.s and Peers. In these circumstances, the British Government knew that carrying out their policy for Northern Rhodesia would require an assertion of their authority, in a matter quite clearly their unique responsibility, over the Federal Government. Permitting the Federal Government to interfere in the February talks, to work behind the scenes to sabotage the work of the constitutional conference, and to conduct a diplomatic offensive over a period of weeks against the Colonial Office, was both stupid and irresponsible. It was stupid because it encouraged the Federal Government to believe that they could force the British Government's hand, it undermined the confidence of the people of the northern protectorate in the honesty and good faith of the Colonial Secretary, and it made more difficult the process of dismantling the Federation. It was irresponsible because it provoked violent reactions in Northern Rhodesia, and it made the preparation of a country's constitution a subject for the skirmishing and skullduggery of politics at their worst. It could not even be commended by the dubious argument that the end justified the means, since the constitution that eventually emerged was in essence that which had been planned from the start, and all that had been achieved by the devious manœuvring was ill-feeling, loss of authority, delay and disillusionment.

I shall deal in the next chapters with British policy towards the Federation as a whole. It remains here to complete the story of Northern Rhodesia's constitution. By mid-June 1961 the scene was set for the definitive announcement of the constitutional framework. Just before it was to be made, the British Government received from the Federal Government proposals which took the fullest advantage of the possibilities for manœuvre around the February scheme for a middle group of 'national' seats. The aim of the Federal proposals was to produce a system that favoured, in elections to these national seats, pro-federal parties–in practice, the UFP itself. In a set of highly sophisticated arguments about delimitation of national constituencies and franchise regulations, Mr. Greenfield included an attack on the spring White Paper's provision that in the national constituencies candidates must secure 'the same prescribed minimum percentage of the votes cast on each roll'. He pointed out that the upper roll, though mainly white, contained some Africans, whereas the lower roll contained virtually no whites. Thus if the national seat elections were to achieve the objective, also stated in the February White Paper, of 'securing substantially increased African representation while maintaining the principle of a non-racial political approach in which political parties are obliged to seek support *from both races*' there was a case for demanding a higher percentage of support from the lower roll than from the upper.

On Friday, June 23, 1961, in a moment of melodrama, Sir Roy Welensky decided at the last moment, following a telephone call from Mr. Duncan Sandys, not to fly to London to enter the lists once more over Northern Rhodesia. On Monday, June 26, when the 'Governor's recommendations', as they were euphemistically called, were published in another White Paper (Cmnd 1423), it was apparent why Sir Roy had felt satisfied. The proposals, which Mr. Macleod had to defend in the House of Commons, differed substantially from the February outline, and the differences

marked a victory for the Federal Government. Under the proposed constitution there were to be forty-five members of the
legislature, of whom fifteen would be elected by the upper roll of
voters, fifteen by the lower roll and fifteen–the 'National members'
–by both rolls combined. The main feature of the scheme was its
extreme complication, and this itself led to misunderstandings, as
we shall see later. In one of its elements, the June 1961 constitutional framework marked a definite step backward. Of the fifteen
national constituencies, four were to be 'mixed twins'–that is,
they were to be reserved for one African and one European
member. And in elections for the national seats, members would
have to obtain a percentage of support from each race ($12\frac{1}{2}$ per
cent or 400 votes, whichever was the less, of the African votes
cast and $12\frac{1}{2}$ per cent or 400 votes, whichever was the less, of the
European votes cast). In the February proposals it had been stated
that candidates must obtain a minimum of support from each roll.
The change meant that, for the first time, purely racial criteria
were to be introduced, and voters would have to be distinguished
by race. For the British Government, this was a clear departure
from principle. It was seen as such by the Rhodesia and Nyasaland
Committee, a body certainly not unsympathetic to Sir Roy Welensky and his policies. Sir Roy himself, however, was quite enthusiastic. In a speech to the Federal Assembly on June 26 he
remarked that the settlement of the constitution would inspire
confidence in the continuing association of the three territories in
the Federation. The constitution proposed, he said, 'has a fair
chance of providing for the continuation of responsible government in Northern Rhodesia'. (In Sir Roy Welensky's political
vocabulary responsible meant pro-federal.) He claimed that the
need to appeal to both races meant that the constitution would
'promote a moderate and non-racial approach to the problems of
government'. Implicitly he claimed credit for the change from a
percentage of both rolls to a percentage of both races.

  This back-pedalling by the British Government from its February decisions must be seen against a background of a deteriorating
situation in Northern Rhodesia itself. Informed observers there
recognized that a change from the grudgingly accepted February
plan to a different one favoured by the Federal Government–and
opposed by both the African parties and the Liberals–made likely
a hardening of attitudes leaving little hope of compromise, and

incidentally little hope of any willingness on the part of Africans to cooperate in talks about a future association with the other federal territories. These reactions must have been known to the British Government. They were certainly known to the press. By acting as they did the Government was deliberately courting serious trouble rather than stand up to the Federal Government.

Furthermore, the June scheme was not even properly worked out. The Northern Rhodesia Government issued a pamphlet headed *Constitutional Changes: The Scheme Explained* which reiterated the provisions of the White Paper that candidates for national seats 'will need to win one-eighth or 400 (whichever is the less) of the European votes cast in the election and one-eighth or 400 (whichever is the less) of the African votes cast in the election'.

A Northern Rhodesia newspaper, *The African Mail*, pointed out that, as each voter in a national constituency would be able to vote for two candidates, $12\frac{1}{2}$ per cent of the European votes would come from 25 per cent of the European voters. On the other hand, 400 African votes would represent probably only 2 per cent of the total African votes cast, the difference deriving from the fact that the total of African voters (mainly on the lower roll) was far larger than the total of European.

This was clearly not the intention, and Mr. Macleod in the House of Commons and the Chief Secretary of Northern Rhodesia in the Legislative Council both pointed out that, in the Chief Secretary's words, ' "votes" here means the "valid ballot papers" which are lodged by European voters or by African voters respectively'. The Chief Secretary also, however, described the article in *The African Mail* as 'a disgraceful and deliberate misrepresentation' though, as *The Times* observed in a leading article, 'It surely cannot be misrepresentation to assume that an official publication means what it says, and the White Paper talks of "votes cast", not of voters or ballot papers.'

The June proposals, which were presented as the British Government's final decision, were, therefore, both ill-conceived and imperfectly shaped. They also, predictably, set off a strong adverse reaction from Mr. Kenneth Kaunda, Sir John Moffat and others who, quite legitimately, saw in them a failure by the British Government to keep faith. Diplomatic manœuvres began once more, this time by Sir John and Mr. Kaunda, both of whom spent a good deal of time in Britain in August and September. During this period, incidents of violence and sabotage occurred in depressing numbers in Northern Rhodesia, carried out by certain members of the United National Independence Party, which was temporarily banned in two of the country's provinces. But it became apparent to more and more people, including the Labour Party, then in opposition, that the June proposals were not acceptable in Northern Rhodesia, and that, even if they were fair, they were not seen to be fair. Influential opinion began to urge the Government to move again, back towards the original February scheme.

On September 14, 1961, in one of his last acts as Colonial Secretary, Mr. Macleod arranged for the issue by the Colonial Office of a statement by Her Majesty's Government. This was a masterpiece of wording carefully drawn up to conceal the fact that it amounted in effect to a climb down. The relevant portion read:

In accordance with their normal practice Her Majesty's Government would have been prepared, before finally implementing their proposals, to consider any reasonable representations about them which those concerned might wish to put forward. They cannot, however, ignore the recent outbreak of grave lawlessness in certain parts of Northern Rhodesia. This carries the risk of serious delay in the constitutional advancement of the Territory, which all are anxious to secure, since it is not possible in such circumstances for any government to give consideration to constitutional issues. Their first task must be to ensure that law and order are maintained.

When, however, in the Governor's judgment, violence and disorder have ceased, HMG will be ready to consider, on the basis of the White Papers and the Secretary of State's statement in the House of Commons on 26th June, any representations within the area where divergences of view persist. HMG would hope that such representations would disclose a prospect of general agreement. In any event, however, they will proceed, after considering them, to take their own final decisions and to publish the necessary instruments to introduce the new constitution and to prepare for a general election.

As might be expected this decision once more to reopen discussions on the Northern Rhodesia constitution displeased the Federal Government, who saw it, rightly, as a move likely to damage the Federation beyond repair. The final word on the constitution did not come until February 28, 1962, and before then the wrangling over details continued. Mr. Maudling, Mr. Macleod's successor at the Colonial Office, visited the territory. Towards the end of February, British ministers met frequently. They had to decide, after all the delays, what the constitution should be, and in particular, they had to decide the method of election to the national seats—the main point at issue, and the point on which would hang the balance of victory in elections under the constitution. Mr. Maudling, having inherited Mr. Macleod's basic framework, and having seen for himself the situation on the spot, was firmly convinced that the decision must be such as to give the Africans a narrow majority. This, clearly, would produce an explosive reaction from Sir Roy Welensky. It would also produce opposition from within the Conservative ranks—and indeed at one stage in February 1962 Mr. Maudling came close to resignation in support of what he knew to be both right and inevitable, in face of doubts among his Cabinet colleagues. The implication of the decision, which was finally endorsed by the Cabinet, was that the Federation was doomed. When the announcement came, Sir Roy Welensky was in London, having arrived breathing fire and fury with his famous speech threatening to 'go the whole hog' to maintain the Federation. On his departure on March 2, he accused the British Government of equivocation and, by implication at least, of perfidy. In view of all that had happened, there is much to be said for his opinion—though little for his policies.

The British Government had laid itself open to Welensky's charges by its refusal to grasp the nettle of decision early enough. Mr. Maudling's approach in February 1962 was precisely the same as Mr. Macleod's in 1961—acceptance of the need for an African majority. The implications of this for the Federation were the same on both occasions, the difference being that the delay had created an acrimonious atmosphere in which any cooperation on future association between the federal territories was most unlikely. Not only had the Government failed to carry its policy through in 1961. It had changed its mind, and gone back on its word, ensuring first the alienation of the Africans and then the —fully justified—realization by the Federal Government that agreements achieved meant virtually nothing. This was not skilful diplomacy, but plain weakness.

The period between the February 1962 decision and the granting of independence to Northern Rhodesia, as Zambia, in October

1964, need not concern us. With the Federation, throughout that period, dying or dead, the protectorate's progress was conventional. In one respect, however, the British Government, this time through Mr. Duncan Sandys, who had become Colonial as well as Commonwealth Secretary, again behaved with incredible folly, and was ready to launch Zambia into independence in conditions which would have imposed a severe strain on the good relations between the new country and Britain. Only the general election of October 1964, and the sensible decision of the new Labour Government to reverse their predecessor's decision at the eleventh hour, retrieved the situation.

The argument concerned the mineral rights of the British South Africa Company (known as 'Chartered') in Northern Rhodesia. The dispute was extremely complex, and many of the assertions made on both sides were challenged. There is no need to go into it all in detail. Essentially the point was that the elected government of what was soon to become Zambia was determined, understandably, that on independence it would own the country's mineral rights. The agreements with Chartered, notably those of 1923 and 1950, were with the British Government (and in the case of the 1950 agreement, with the colonial Northern Rhodesian Government as a third party). The question of compensation, the Zambians argued, was for the British Government to settle, though they let it be known that they would contribute. The company (which has since changed its name and its form) fought fiercely, if not for the continuance of its rights, then for a large sum in compensation. The negotiations were conducted, for the British Government, by Lord Dilhorne, the Lord Chancellor. At the end of September 1964, less than a month before Zambia's independence, the negotiations broke down, the British Government insisting that the question of compensation was primarily a matter for the Northern Rhodesian Government and the company, though the British Government were ready to use their good offices. On behalf of the Zambians, Mr. Arthur Wina, the Finance Minister, made clear that his Government which held that the rights were invalid, and accepted no residual responsibility, would refuse to honour any obligations to Chartered, and would extinguish the rights after independence, without payment of compensation, making a change in the constitution which would be necessary in order to do this.

Even in the City, many people felt that Chartered's case was weak, and that the company had received enough money already during its years in the territory, particularly since it had never actually been involved in the production of copper but simply owned the mineral rights. In a leader of September 30, 1964 *The Financial Times* wrote, 'Zambia will naturally be anxious about its international credit. But investors would do well to judge it by its attitude to foreign companies other than Chartered.' In *The Guardian* on October 1, 1964 Patrick Keatley, the Commonwealth correspondent and the author of a book on the Federation,* discussed the anxieties of other firms with interests in Zambia, including Rhodesian Selection Trust, Rhodesian Anglo-American (the two big copper companies) and Booker Brothers. Keatley wrote:

> None of these has been associated in any way with the campaign of the Chartered Company. If anything, they have long ago been disenchanted with the B.S.A. policy, regarding it as leading . . . to a head-on clash with an African nationalist government at the moment of its coming to power.

There was widespread sympathy for the Zambians' attitude. To enter independence with the country's main source of wealth in alien hands would be intolerable for any government. Furthermore, it was clear that whatever the legal position might be–and it was a matter of controversy–not only did the company's position appear weak, but the British Government's moral obligation to settle the issue seemed strong. The agreements with Chartered had, after all, been made by the British Government without reference to anything like a representative government. Politically, if the mineral rights dispute persisted into independence, the picture of the City's relationship with the under-developed countries would be bad, and at the same time an act of sequestration by Zambia would inevitably sour Zambian–British relations in a part of Africa where the Southern Rhodesian difficulties, if nothing else, made good relations important.

In other words, by allowing the controversy to continue and by refusing to settle it reasonably, the Conservative Government, on the eve of the general election, was guilty of a further utterly irresponsible act. The Order in Council promulgating the inde-

* *The Politics of Partnership*, Penguin, 1963.

pendence constitution was signed on October 15, but was not published until October 21, only three days before independence. During the weekend of October 17 and 18 Mr. Arthur Bottomley, having taken over the portfolio of Commonwealth Affairs, had to study the whole complex question as a matter of urgency, and finally, on the very eve of independence day, the dispute was settled satisfactorily. The fact that such desperate last-minute action was necessary was typical of the indecision and uncertainty that marked the whole approach to Northern Rhodesia's affairs of both Mr. Macmillan's and Sir Alec Douglas-Home's governments.

Chapter 8

Central African Failure

THE problem for the British Government in Kenya was to bring about the change from rule by the Colonial Office to rule by an elected local majority and at the same time to change the balance of political power within the territory so that it lay in African rather than European hands. It took a long time for the basic decision to be made, but when it had been, the European minority could do little but protest. In Central Africa, the same problem existed, with an important difference. There, as a creature of British policy, the Federation of Rhodesia and Nyasaland stood as an intermediate bulwark between Whitehall and the individual white man. Implementing the policy of introducing majority rule –the policy of the wind of change–was complicated by the existence of the Federal Government fighting a strong rearguard action to preserve the balance of power as it was. A further, and connected, complication, was the traditional constitutional position of Southern Rhodesia, which became a self-governing colony (with power in the hands of the white minority) in 1923, which traditionally enjoyed many of the privileges of independence, such as for example the right of its prime ministers, in pre-federal days, to attend Commonwealth Prime Ministers' meetings, and which passed on its fundamental political attitudes to the Federal Government. The Federation, after ten stormy years of existence as a quasi-state, is extinct, a monument to the failure of an idea, and in the history of Africa a mere incident in the path of change. In its conception, the Federation was one of the worst examples of British governmental folly. Its own leaders proved to be unable, if not unwilling, to shape their policies wisely to contemporary conditions. For the final three years of the Federation's existence, they blustered and blundered, clinging grimly to unrealistic aims, their misdirected sense of self-preservation making inevitable their own political destruction. In the same period the British Government, having been forced into the realization that the infant they

104

had sired, though it had reached a troublesome adolescence, was fated not to achieve adulthood, temporized and wavered, uttered half hints where clear statements were required, and finally delivered the *coup de grâce* in a way which earned them justifiably the calumny of the Federal Government.

The Federation failed because it never enjoyed the support of the Africans who are the majority of the three territories which formed it—Southern Rhodesia, Northern Rhodesia (now Zambia) and Nyasaland (now Malawi). The strength of African feelings, particularly in the northern territories, about any form of association with white-ruled Southern Rhodesia, was well-known and long attested. The Federation came into being in 1953, but already in 1939 the Bledisloe Commission, set up to examine the possibility of association, had considered closer unity to be desirable in principle but thought no active steps should be taken at that stage to achieve it because of the extent of African opposition.

By the time, in 1951, that the idea of federation began to be seriously discussed, African political opinion throughout the continent had matured with the experience of the Second World War. In 1951 a conference took place of officials from the British Government and the governments of Southern Rhodesia, Northern Rhodesia and Nyasaland to discuss the future relationship of the three territories. The officials recommended that there should be a close political association and their views were put forward by Mr. James Griffiths, Colonial Secretary in the Labour Government then in power, as a basis of discussion. It at once became apparent that African feelings were still strongly opposed to association with Southern Rhodesia, and these feelings were widely reported and commented on by newspapers and authoritative observers. In 1951 the British Labour Government fell, and the Conservatives came to power. They were to stay in office through two further elections for thirteen years, surviving the Suez crisis, but the Conservative Government of the early 1950s was of a very different character and worked in very different conditions from that defeated by Labour in 1964. It was a government, for one thing, in which the concept of empire was still alive. This was, after all, the period before even Ghana had stirred far towards independence.

The Conservative Colonial Secretary, Mr. Oliver Lyttelton (now Lord Chandos) took over with enthusiasm the scheme for a central African federation, and significantly changed the emphasis of discussion. African objections were played down. The economic advantages of federation were stressed. The Federal framework was worked out in the absence of African representatives on the principle that if they would not recognize what was good for them, someone else would have to make the decisions. African mistrust was inevitably increased, particularly as one of the leading partici- pants in the discussions was Lord Malvern (then Sir Godfrey Huggins), Prime Minister of Southern Rhodesia, a man who made no secret of his view that Africans would for the foreseeable future be very much the junior partners in the body politic of the new state. I have already mentioned his notorious 'horse and rider' remark. It was not an isolated instance. When campaigning in Southern Rhodesia for white support for the federation—and there was a good deal of opposition to it—he reassured his audience that they need have no fear that there would be a black parliament for the next fifty or sixty years.

Such things were warning signs that should have been heeded by the British Government. It should have been obvious both that African fears were genuine and that, given the political leaders who would take power in the proposed federation, they were fully justified. The first error of the British Government in dealing with the affairs of Central Africa was to ignore these warning signs. It was an error that was repeated continually throughout the dismal history of the Federation, with successive failures to take the measure of the Federal Government or to stand by perfectly clear and simple principles. In the early days, before the Federation was formed, there was an apparent inability to appreciate the nature of African objections. Philip Mason, in his book *Year of Decision: Rhodesia and Nyasaland* 1960* discusses this as follows:

Another point of the first importance was hardly revealed in news- paper comment at this stage. But it had been noted during the Bledisloe inquiry and nothing since had occurred to modify it. The African objec- tion was not only to a policy in native affairs nor to any legal or con- stitutional point; it could not be met by economic argument. There was objection to a look in the eye, discernible not in every European but in perhaps nine out of ten, a look that was taken by the African to mean 'they do not like us or want to mix with us'. That this was what the look meant was confirmed by almost every social institution in both the

* Oxford University Press, 1960.

Rhodesias and it led most articulate Africans to a simple calculation of how these institutions could most quickly be changed. This, it seemed to them, was more likely to happen under Colonial Office rule than under what they believed would be the rule of Southern Rhodesia.

Articulate Africans, who were far more numerous than ever the federal leaders admitted even in the last days of the Federation, wanted political power, and, incidentally, an end to racial discrimination. It has been common for defenders of the Federation, in Central Africa and in Britain and elsewhere, to emphasize the material benefits which it brought and was likely to bring. The economic potential of the Federation as compared with any of the individual territories was seen as a conclusive argument in its favour. The same sort of argument is frequently used by people discussing other African countries. It is certainly used by the defenders of the Verwoerd régime in South Africa. Essentially, the argument runs, independence tends to bring a worsening rather than an improvement in economic conditions, therefore 'the African would prefer to remain unindependent'. The argument is entirely specious. The desire to run one's own affairs is a natural human instinct, not just an African quirk, and it is not determined or diminished by economic considerations. Members of resistance movements in occupied Europe during the Second World War, for example, could no doubt have led more comfortable lives had they accepted alien rule.

In 1953 the Federation was born, therefore, with inauspicious omens. Insufficient provision had been made for African political advancement and the strong African feelings against the scheme were ignored. In spite of all the signs to the contrary, it was assumed in British Government circles that the Federation's political leaders would voluntarily draw Africans into the local corridors of power. Instead of making African political advancement a condition of yielding some of Britain's authority to the Federal Government, instead of putting pressure on the Federal leaders to liberalize their system, and introduce policies that might gradually win the approval of the population, the British Government allowed themselves to be bemused by the ideas of 'kith and kinship' and talk of 'partnership'. Finally, having failed even to try persuasion, and having for a number of years swallowed the Federal line, the latter-day Conservatives recognized that they had backed the wrong horse. Sensibly enough, they decided to change their policy. Even then, however, they proved unwilling to indulge in straight talk. The failure, in other words, was threefold. First, the Government imposed Federation against the will of the people. Secondly, they allowed the Federal Government to pursue policies that did nothing to justify the power that had been given to them. Finally, when dismemberment became inevitable, they failed to deal honestly with the Federal Government whose demise they were planning.

The detailed history of the Federation is outside the scope of this book. I want to mention one or two aspects of it which illustrate the thesis I am arguing. The first is the treatment of the African Affairs Board. This board was set up under the original constitution as a means of safeguarding African interests. It was a compromise resulting from long argument, and it was not a particularly good one, even if it had been accepted in a cooperative spirit by all concerned. In fact the Federal leaders made it clear that they had no intention of allowing its teeth to bite. The board's function was 'to make representations on matters considered desirable in the interests of Africans and to draw attention to any Bill which subjects Africans to conditions, restrictions or disabilities to which Europeans are not also subjected'. If such 'differentiating measures' were proposed, the African Affairs Board had power to require their reservation for the British Parliament. The first major issue taken up by the board was the Constitution Amendment Bill of 1957 which altered the Federal franchise in a way which would reduce the proportion of African parliamentary representation. This Bill and the Federal Electoral Bill, also reserved by the board, were held by the British Parliament not to be discriminatory – a decision which owed more to the Conservative Government's desire to strike a bargain with Sir Roy Welensky, by this time Federal Prime Minister, than to an impartial examination of the Bills' merits. Such value as the African Affairs Board had as a means of reassuring African opinion was thus cut away. Sir John Moffat, the board's chairman, resigned.

The second point I would mention is the 1957 'bargain' referred to above. It was made during talks in London between the British Government and Sir Roy on the Federal franchise and other constitutional matters. It was one-sided, since it consisted largely of concessions by the British to the Federal Government. It handed over a wide measure of responsibility for external affairs to the Federal Government. It included an acceptance of the principle that there should be no secession of any territory from the Federation. Most important, it set out the principle recorded in the communiqué that followed the talks in the following terms:

The United Kingdom Government recognizes the existence of a convention, applicable to the present stage of the constitutional evolution of the Federation, whereby the United Kingdom Government in practice does not initiate any legislation to amend or repeal any Federal Act or to deal with any matter included within the competence of the Federal Legislature, except at the request of the Federal Government.

In other words, the British Government voluntarily gave up effective control over any of the internal affairs of the Federation – and thereby made it difficult in the future to do anything to induce a more liberal attitude to the all-important question of African political power. This convention, incidentally, had already been held to apply to pre-Federal Southern Rhodesia, which, it should be remembered, had been granted internal self-government in an era when the dangers of handing over power to a white minority were not so well recognized as they should have been by the 1950s. In the period of the final death throes of the Federation, the existence of this convention, and the interpretation placed upon it by the Federal Government, became a stick to beat the back of the British Government, and the crux of charges of perfidy levelled at British Ministers. It was a stick which the British Government voluntarily placed in Federal hands.

Another point to which I want to draw attention is the failure of the policy of partnership and the multi-racial political system to appeal to the African majority in the Federation. Partnership soon became a dirty word among Africans. It is easy to see why when one looks at Lord Malvern's approach to it. For the Federation's supporters in the early days, however, the concept of partnership was one of the great merits of the federal ideal. It was at best a woolly philosophy. In any case, neither Lord Malvern nor Sir Roy Welensky left any room for doubt that the Africans, though in the majority, were to be permanent junior partners. The favourite formula was that government should remain in 'civilized and responsible' hands, and Sir Roy made it clear that however 'civilized and responsible' he became the African could 'never hope

H

to dominate the partnership. He can achieve equal standing but not go beyond it.' Equality, that is to say, was to be given on a purely racial basis. White men, though in a small minority, were never to have to compete on really equal terms with their fellow citizens.

In practice, even the limited goal of advance to parity of races was never remotely in sight. One of the most obvious ways in which the Federal leaders could have demonstrated their good faith, and one which they would have adopted had they possessed an ounce of statesmanship, would have been the appointment of a number of African ministers to the Federal cabinet. This was never done. The nearest they got to it was the appointment of Mr. Jasper Savanhu as a parliamentary Secretary–one black junior minister in a white man's club. In 1962 Mr. Savanhu resigned both from the government and the United Federal Party, stating when he did so that the Federal Government had failed to implement its policy of partnership.

The policy of partnership was not implemented because the Federal leaders were in fact dedicated to the preservation of white supremacy. The retention of traditional privilege is an understandable desire of any privileged class, but for Sir Roy Welensky and his colleagues to act as they did illustrated one of the basic weaknesses of the Federation–its lack of leadership. The constant controversies that surrounded the Federation and its relationship with Britain have clouded what seems to me to be this key fact, and in underlining it I do not wish to be misunderstood. Sir Roy Welensky is a man of many great qualities, not least the ability to take a battering. He is charming. His relationship with the press, even the press which disagreed with him, was always good. He likes plain blunt talk, and he has always been ready to take as well as give. I personally had a good deal to do with him over a period of several years, at a time when *The Times* was severely critical of his policies. I never found him anything but courteous, even when under the strongest pressures and stresses. In sheer ability and personality Sir Roy stood head and shoulders above the dismal mediocrity of his government colleagues.

Here again, I would not wish to be misunderstood. The white population of Southern Rhodesia is roughly the equivalent in numbers of that of the city of Kingston upon Hull. Add the white population of the other two territories, and you still have only a large British city. It would be surprising if in the average large city you found sufficient men to form a government and an opposition, to staff a bench of judges, to fill the whole range of professions, to run a number of municipalities and to provide both a business and a farming community. Not surprisingly, such men were not available in the Federation, and one of the errors of the British Government and much of British public opinion was to assume that the government machine of the Federation was a sophisticated structure run by people of the calibre found in any British Government, whatever its political complexion. Parenthetically, it seems to me that the same error has been made in British dealings with Southern Rhodesia. Inevitably, Sir Roy Welensky stood out; but that is not to say that he was a great statesman. Few men are, and it is no discredit to him to remark that though he was often an excellent tactician, he never managed to take the broad strategic view and adopt the policies that might just possibly have made the Federation work. The explanation is not hard to find. He was a politician of strictly limited aims. He gripped firmly on what he and his supporters possessed. He wanted to preserve the *status quo*, but he never seemed to realize that in politics there is no *status quo*. He could, and did, strike attitudes. Having made up his mind, he could stick to it doggedly. What he seemed incapable of doing was to change his mind as circumstances changed, to adapt himself to a political background that resembled a kaleidoscope more than a set-piece tableau. He was, in a word, insensitive to change (just as Mr. Ian Smith of Southern Rhodesia and his colleagues–with far less ability than Sir Roy–are today insensitive). By this insensitivity he failed to perceive what had to be done and accepted.

I have mentioned earlier the confused thinking that has existed on the subject of multi-racialism. Multi-racialism was adopted by the United Federal Party for quite understandable reasons; if it worked, it would be a way of keeping race out of politics in the sense that Africans would think of themselves as voters or politicians, not as African voters or politicians. If the vote, and political power, were to go to people because of their qualifications rather than their colour, it was easy to ensure that the Europeans would continue to dominate, simply because the qualifications, imposed by the existing white *élite*, were European qualifications. Strictly speaking, multi-racialism means giving political rights to different races *as such*–the system tried briefly in Kenya, as I have described above. In the Federation, the element of pure multi-racialism was the arrangement (in both the initial legislature and in that following constitutional changes in 1957 and 1958) for the election of special African representatives, and Europeans representing Africans. The Federal franchise, on the other hand, made no racial provisions. There were, after 1958, two electoral rolls, with income, property and educational qualifications. In practice, the qualifications were such that the more influential position was assured to Europeans, whereas Africans would have far more difficulty in earning the right to vote.

The Federal Government became more and more touchy on the subject of multi-racialism, as I discovered by chance from something that I wrote in 1961. Soon after the publication of the February 1961 White Paper on Northern Rhodesia's constitution (see previous chapter) I read a set of statements made by British M.P.s who had returned from a visit to the Federation organized by Voice and Vision Ltd., the public relations firm employed at great expense as advisers by the Federal Government (whose activities, incidentally, most of my journalistic colleagues and I viewed with great wariness). I noticed in these statements that the terms multi-racial and non-racial were used as if they were interchangeable. Mr. Macleod in his White Paper, on the other hand, had deliberately rejected the term multi-racial. He had written: 'It is not a term that I favour: the aim of policy which I recommend to you is that of non-racialism.' I wrote an article pointing out that the word multi-racial, in relation to the Federation's policies, had come into disrepute particularly among Africans because, although multi-racialism ignored colour as such and concentrated on voting qualifications, it in practice provided for the dominance of the white voter. I pointed out that in a non-racial political system racial differences played no part in democratic processes. The United Kingdom's political system, for example, was non-racial. Inevitably, under such a system, a large racial majority is bound to dominate the political set-up – by natural process, not by constitutional privilege. I then quoted various speeches by Sir Roy Welensky in which he had said the policy in the Federation aimed at the development of a multi-racial state but, on another occasion, 'a non-racial approach' which, he said, he wanted to see enshrined in Federal affairs. I then explained that by no stretch of the imagination could the UFP's policies be described as non-racialism, since their effect-temporarily perhaps-was to secure the dominance of a minority race.

Soon after this article appeared I was approached by the Federal High Commissioner, Mr. (later Sir Albert) Robinson, who told me I had got things all wrong. Two years later I discovered that one of *The Times*'s local correspondents in Central Africa had been asked what was the meaning of writing such an article. The irritated reaction of the Federal authorities confirmed the truth of what I had intended to convey, namely that multi-racialism was in practice synonymous with white minority domination. It was not surprising that multi-racialism failed to appeal to the African majority.

I have, I hope, written enough to demonstrate that the method of the Federation's birth, and the policies and practices of its leaders, made its failure likely, if not inevitable. Further, having made a serious error of judgment at the time of its foundation, the British Government compounded their error thereafter, by failing themselves to reassure the Africans (the incident of the African Affairs Board) and by permitting the Federal Government to evade British control (the 1957 bargain).

By 1960 the certainty of failure was becoming difficult to ignore. A number of events combined to emphasize the need for important decisions. One was the publication in 1959 of the Devlin Report on the disturbances in Nyasaland. This, as I have shewn in a previous chapter, was highly critical of aspects of British rule in that protectorate, and because it was a document politically embarrassing to the Conservatives at a moment when they were about to go to the country in the 1959 election, the report was formally rejected, for the Government which had appointed the commission, by Mr. Lennox-Boyd (now Lord Boyd), who was Colonial Secretary. The decision to reject it was by any standards a depressing example of the triumph of expediency over principle. The lesson of Devlin, however, was not entirely lost, and after winning the election the Conservatives, as we have seen, changed their colonial policy and appointed Mr. Iain Macleod to conduct it. They also appointed a Commission under the chairmanship of Lord Monckton to investigate the Federation and advise on its future. The appointment and the terms of reference of the Monckton Commission were a matter of great controversy. All that need concern us here is the report which they issued in 1960, and which was published as a

White Paper (Cmnd 1148) in October. It stated quite unequivocally that 'the strength of African opposition in the northern territories is such that Federation cannot, in our view, be maintained in its present form'. The Commission recommended 'prompt and far-reaching reforms'. The British Government should announce their intention to permit any territory to secede from the Federation. Racial discrimination should be made illegal. The name 'Federation', the focus of opposition, should be changed. The commission recognized 1957 as the turning point from which opposition began to increase rather than diminish, and they declared: 'To hold the Federation together by force we regard as out of the question.'

Already by early 1960 feeling within the Federation had become increasingly anti-Federal. The African nationalists, of course, opposed it strongly, but apart from them, the Central Africa Party (led by Sir John Moffat) had become thoroughly disillusioned, and in Southern Rhodesia the territorial branch of the United Federal Party was beginning to move towards the position long held by a substantial minority of the (white) Southern Rhodesian voters, and to see Federation as an imposition rather than an advantage, given the trend of events.

One reflection of this trend was Mr. Macmillan's 'wind of change' tour and the speeches he made during it. At various points in his African journey he gave an assurance that British protection for Northern Rhodesia and Nyasaland would remain until their people expressed a wish to enter an independent Federation; he explained that the popular will could be expressed only when a territory was fully self-governing; he made clear that the way forward for the Federation required careful consideration. And in general he reaffirmed the British Government's new determination to encourage majority rule in the territories under its control and not to hand over power to racial minorities.

In December 1960, two months after the publication of the Monckton Report, and at a moment when the lessons of the wind of change tour had had nearly a year to sink in, a conference opened in London to review the Federation. Provision for a review was written into the constitution. It was to take place between seven and nine years from the foundation of the Federation. By calling it in 1960, the British Government were choosing the earliest possible moment. The atmosphere in which it was held was quite different from that which the founding fathers of the Federation would have expected. Nyasaland had its new constitution promising African rule. The Monckton Report had appeared. The list of delegates to the conference included the nationalist leaders, men such as Kenneth Kaunda, who only a few months before had been written down as agitators representing no one but themselves. The Federation, in a word, was doomed.

The 1960 conference was abortive. It was adjourned *sine die* – and no day was ever named for its resumption. Northern Rhodesia began its journey to independence, described in the previous chapter. Nyasaland's election in 1961 confirmed what the constitutional agreement of 1960 has implied – that the country would be ruled by an anti-Federal African party. Nyasaland's right to secede was accepted in December 1962, in a statement in the House of Commons by Mr. R. A. Butler (now Lord Butler), then in charge of Central African affairs. Northern Rhodesia's secession right was accepted in April 1963. In July 1963 Mr. Butler presided at a conference at Victoria Falls (on the frontier between the Rhodesias) at which the funeral arrangements were made. On the last day of 1963, it ceased to exist. That, in bare outline, is the story from the moment, in 1960, when the impossibility of keeping the Federation in being became clearly apparent to all but the most dedicated disciples. Until quite a late stage, there were reasonable hopes that some looser form of economic association could be evolved to rise from the ashes of political union. These hopes proved unrealistic; Southern Rhodesia's policies and her position as a hated object of enmity for African nationalists throughout the continent saw to that. That radical changes would be necessary, and were inevitable, was known by the British Government even before the 1960 conference met. If confirmation of this is required, it is to be found in Mr. Macleod's approach to the Northern Rhodesia constitutional talks, but in any case, the evidence discussed by the Monckton Commission could no longer be ignored. Sir Roy Welensky, on the other hand, did not accept the inevitability of radical change. Each effort to make changes he opposed fiercely. Relations between him and the British Government, as we have seen in the previous chapter, got worse and worse.

This difference in approach, combined with the personality of Sir Roy, ensured that the British Government's task in achieving the necessary metamorphosis would be difficult. That was all the more a reason for deciding the aims, stating them, and sticking to them, and above all, for leaving Sir Roy in no doubt what they were–and facing the outburst of rage which the knowledge would certainly provoke from him. Yet straightforwardness was the last thing the British Government shewed.

Throughout 1961, as we have seen, the future of the Federation hung on the constitutional developments that were being worked out for Northern Rhodesia, and the parallel discussions, during a part of the period, on Southern Rhodesia's constitution. One of the main difficulties which the British Government suffered was the fact that two British Departments, the Commonwealth Relations Office and the Colonial Office, were responsible for different aspects of the problem. The C.R.O. was in charge of relations with the Federation, and with Southern Rhodesia. The C.O. was responsible for Northern Rhodesia and Nyasaland in their internal developments. The complication of this dual responsibility was increased by the different approach of the two departments–and perhaps even more by the different personalities of the Secretaries of State. There was much circumstantial evidence which led any close observer of events to conclude that Mr. Duncan Sandys and Mr. Iain Macleod were at daggers drawn. Certainly, at a time when Macleod had recognized that Northern Rhodesia was going to have an African Government–on a non-racial system–Sandys was still a convinced multi-racialist, and a believer in the policies of Sir Edgar Whitehead, Prime Minister of Southern Rhodesia (whose particular brand of the United Federal Party philosophy, incidentally, proved too liberal for his electorate, who replaced the UFP by the Rhodesian Front). Certainly, too, the personalities of the two men were very different, and at various stages of the protracted argument in the February-to-June 1961 stage of the Northern Rhodesian constitutional battle Mr. Sandys gave the impression that he, rather than Mr. Macleod, wanted to be taken as the main progenitor of the constitutional framework.

It is tempting to overstress this idea of a split between the C.R.O. and the Colonial Office–and their respective political masters. But when all allowances are made, the fact remains that the two men found it difficult to pull in the same direction, and the Federation's relations with the British Government were correspondingly worse than they need have been. Recognition that the double responsibility did not work came in March 1962, when Mr. R. A. Butler took full charge of central African affairs from both his colleagues (Mr. Sandys and, by now, Mr. Maudling). The appointment of Mr. Butler was a turning point. Before considering it, it is worth having a slightly longer look at the situation up to March 1962.

Nearly a year before, in May 1961, Mr. A. E. P. Robinson, (later Sir Albert), newly arrived in London as Federal High Commissioner, with the tasks of trying to encourage investment, to keep the Federation in being, and to prevent the British Government from diluting the UFP approach, was bemoaning the difficulty of dealing with a government which hardly knew its own mind, and which suffered from a split personality over Central Africa. He quickly recognized that one of his problems was going to be the refusal of the British Government to state what their policy was. Did they or did they not intend to support the Federation? Soon after his arrival, he was pressing for an answer to that question, which supports my argument that the British Government would have been wise to give it, whatever uproar would have temporarily resulted, rather than sit waiting to be overtaken by events.

By September 1961 – the time, it will be recalled, when Mr. Macleod announced the British Government's readiness to receive further representations on Northern Rhodesia's constitution – the Colonial Office side of the split personality at least was finding encouragement in the fact that the UFP was not represented in either the Nyasaland or the Northern Rhodesia legislature. (They had been defeated in Nyasaland, and, as explained above, had resigned in Northern Rhodesia.) Furthermore, Sir Roy Welensky's criticisms of the September 1961 statement were seen in the Colonial Office as being helpful. So, indeed, they were, but as no statement of a change in British policy had been made to Sir Roy or his representative, the Colonial Office were exulting in the discomfiture of a government with which they were ostensibly cooperating.

At about the same period Mr. Duncan Sandys, looking at the future of the Federation as a whole, which was of course his responsibility, began to recognize – what should have been obvious for a year – that the chances of keeping Nyasaland in the Federation were slim. He still seemed to believe that federation was what the Africans really wanted–though with the proviso that it must be an association with far fewer and weaker powers at the centre. In fact, every African nationalist utterance suggested that no association even remotely recognizable as the successor of the hated Federation would stand a chance of acceptance. If any inter-territorial links were to be forged, they would have to be within the context of pan-African thinking on unity–and, as subsequent events have shewn, there has been little success anywhere in the continent in giving tangible territorial form to ideas of unity.

In the autumn of 1961, as it happened, the British Government's thinking on the Federation came to a halt, because of the growing crisis in the neighbouring Congo which had important repercussions throughout the Central African region. As we have seen, Northern Rhodesia, by virtue of the September 1961 statement, was poised on the brink of decision, but the decision was delayed until the next year. For the rest, in so far as there was a policy worthy of the name, it was to play for time while the Congo cauldron bubbled. It is easy to see why. Sir Roy Welensky, who had in practice acquired wide powers of independent action in external affairs as well as the internal running of his country, had strong views about the secession of Katanga under Mr. Tshombe's leadership. He was a supporter of Tshombe, whom he summed up in his book *Welensky's 4000 Days** as 'a remarkable man, honest, brave and highly intelligent, though I realize that this is not the conventional view'. He was rightly concerned about any disturbances in the Congo, and particularly in Katanga, which borders Zambia. He felt that the United Nations in the Congo behaved foolishly and irresponsibly. He felt that the British Government should grant recognition to the 'independent state of Katanga'.

In fairness, I should declare my own views. I went to Katanga in July 1961, shortly before the first U.N. attack on Mr. Tshombe's Government in September 1961. I had the opportunity to see there Dr. Conor Cruise O'Brien, then the chief U.N. representative in Katanga, and soon to be the leading figure in the 'Katanga war'. At the time, it seemed to me:

(a) that Tshombe was nobody's stooge, as people then liked to depict him;

* Collins, 1964.

(b) that in a country where chaos was becoming endemic, his Katangese Government was appreciably more effective than the central Leopoldville Government;

(c) that Dr. O'Brien's interpretation of his role as the representative of the U.N. was unwise, to put it mildly; and

(d) that the U.N. itself, in its military operations in Katanga, was inept (and in the September 1961 incident was exceeding its mandate; the mandate was later changed).

I appreciate that to be a 'Tshombe man' was at that time eccentric, particularly as I share few of the other views on African affairs of the average Tshombe supporter. Subsequent events, and Mr. Tshombe's subsequent activities, however, have not caused me to change my assessment. He seems to me to be the ablest of the Congo's politicians, with the possible exception of Patrice Lumumba, who was killed before he could really shew his talents.

I have made this digression to indicate that I agree with Sir Roy in many of his assessments of Mr. Tshombe and the Congo situation in 1961-2. The British Government, however, found them an acute embarrassment, not least because their own policy on the Congo and Mr. Tshombe's position was in a state of flux. There were grave doubts in Whitehall about the wisdom of the U.N's behaviour and the actions of Dr. O'Brien. At the same time, it was obviously difficult for the British Government to pursue a policy in direct contravention of the majority of the U.N.–including the United States, who were strongly (and in my view quite mistakenly) backing Mr. Adoula in the belief that he could bring some order to the country. The British Government was in an unenviable position. By Sir Roy Welensky and his colleagues they were bullied and criticized for not standing out against aspects of U.N. policy, for not backing Mr. Tshombe and for allowing the Federation's interests to suffer as a result of happenings in the Congo. By a large section of world opinion, they were accused of supporting Mr. Tshombe and hindering the United Nations in their efforts at reunification. The Congo, unfortunately, was, and still is to some extent, a subject on which opinions are emotional rather than logical. Above all, the British Government suffered by being identified with Sir Roy Welensky, who made no secret not only of his support for Mr. Tshombe but of his distaste for the U.N.

The situation amounted to this. The Federal Government, as a result of the 'convention' and of the interpretation which had been put over the years on the federal constitution, was in a position to pursue a foreign policy which was not simply independent of Britain's, but actually in some key respects opposed to it. To take just one example, when the Federation was accused of smuggling arms to the Tshombe 'rebels' the question arose of allowing U.N. observers to watch the Federal frontier. Diplomatically it would have been sensible for Britain–whose legal international responsibility this was–to accept the suggestion, particularly as both the British and Federal Government insisted that there was nothing to hide. In Whitehall, the advice was to agree, but Sir Roy flatly refused, and made public counter-accusations of atrocities, against the U.N. The Federal Government made it quite clear that the British Government's role in U.N.–Rhodesian relations was that of a postman.

Sir Roy's feelings about the Congo began to colour all his thinking on the Federation. One of his objections to the trend which he discerned in Britain's policy towards Northern Rhodesia in 1961–2, for example, was that the British Government were planning to put anti-Tshombe elements in power in Lusaka. The British Government were in fact certainly not thinking in these terms. Their approach to the Northern Rhodesia constitution, already discussed fully above, might best be described as erratic realism, brought finally to fruition by Mr. Maudling who had entered the colonial field with great ability but a great absence of knowledge, and who always gave the impression–also, for example, in the Kenya conference of early 1962–that he was more concerned with finding a settlement than a solution. His heart was obviously in the right place, and he was in any case far too intelligent to believe that the Lord Salisbury approach to the Federation was even remotely workable. He never seemed, however, to enjoy the Colonial Office or to find it an adequate outlet for his particular talents. He held office there for only a short time, but even if he had stayed longer, he would hardly have earned a place among the ranks of great Colonial Secretaries. The British Government's approach to the Federation at this time was still a kind of paralysis. Ministers were more and more accepting that the Federation was doomed. Mr. Maudling, while making the final preparations for the Northern Rhodesia announcement, was trying to establish what sort of support there would be for Sir Roy Welensky in the showdown that seemed inevitable. The Government were still refusing, however, to take up any firm position. At the end of Sir Roy's visit to London in February–March 1962 to protest about the Northern Rhodesia decision, they began to put out surreptitiously the idea that the Federation had always been primarily an economic union and that that was where its future value lay–as if in an economic union the crucial political question of power could be simply ignored. They missed the opportunity provided by Sir Roy just before he left London, when he complained of lack of British backing and said:

I have . . . asked them [the British Prime Minister and the Secretaries of State for Commonwealth Relations and the Colonies] to tell me what is their conception of the future of the Federation, but I have never had a satisfactory or unequivocal reply. One of my main complaints against the British Government is that they have done little or nothing to establish or maintain faith in the Federation.

As Sir Roy made clear a few days later in a speech to the Federal Parliament:

We look to the implementation of the spirit and letter of the convention subscribed to in April, 1957, by Her Majesty's Government and the Federal Government in which these words occur:

'The purpose of this conference is to review the constitution in the light of the experience gained since the inception of the Federation and in addition to agree on constitutional advances which may be made. In this latter context the conference will consider a programme for the attainment of such a status as would enable the Federation to become eligible for full membership of the Commonwealth.'

The conference referred to was, of course, the Federal review conference, which had met and achieved nothing, and whose resumption by this time no sensible observer thought in the least likely. Whether Sir Roy really believed that the purpose to which he referred could still be achieved is a moot point. The important thing is that in the absence of any overt indication of British Government thinking to the contrary, he had grounds for making the statement. It could be argued that Sir Roy was being uncooperative and unrealistic. It could be claimed–it was in fact claimed in my hearing by a British cabinet minister–that the best course was to allow Sir Roy to say what he liked and destroy himself politically in the process. This was hardly an honourable or courageous way of tackling the question. Nor was it helpful to Britain's international standing, because what Sir Roy said could reasonably be taken as reflecting British policy for the Federation, still, after all, Britain's responsibility.

On March 8, 1962, Sir Roy, speaking to the Federal Parliament (the speech in which he announced his intention to recommend the dissolution of Parliament and the holding of a Federal election) said he was determined to put a stop to 'erosion of the Federal structure'. In Britain at about the same time, Mr. Macmillan at last decided to take positive action to hasten the process of erosion. Central Africa was taken out of the hands of the two Secretaries of State. Mr. R. A. Butler was appointed to preside over the Federation's last rites.

Chapter 9

Mr Butler Performs the Last Rites

THE appointment of Mr. Butler to take charge of Central African affairs marked the first practical move by the British Government to evolve and carry out a policy based on the facts of the situation. Until then, as I have tried to shew, there were *ad hoc* decisions, piecemeal approaches to the Central African problem. Perhaps inevitably, with responsibility shared uneasily by two British Government departments, the whole matter sometimes seemed to be treated as a kind of game. 'Scoring off Welensky' was a popular sport, particularly for the Colonial Office. When Sir Roy Welensky decided to dissolve the Federal Parliament and hold an election in early 1962, his decision was greeted with glee in parts of Whitehall where it was seen, rightly, as a major tactical error by Sir Roy. (In fact, the Federal election was virtually boycotted by all except the United Federal Party, who were returned to office, but could no longer claim to be representative.) There were sighs of relief because Sir Roy, the apparently firm rock on which Federal policies were built, the formidable opponent, suddenly turned out not to be quite such an immutable fixture.

With Mr. Butler's arrival on the scene, it at once became clear that the Government at last intended to clarify its ideas. Right at the beginning of Mr. Butler's term of office, he made it plain that the Government would act strictly in accordance with the pledge made to the people of the two northern territories in the preamble to the Federal constitution. He emphasized the importance of popular consent, and consultation with the people, before any constitutional moves were made, and he underlined what the Monckton Report had said on this. Realistically, he avoided from the start references to any future federation, preferring instead to speak of a form of association between the territories. Even that, he recognized quickly, might be impossible; the forces of African nationalism, might prove too strong (as, in the event, they did).

By May certainly, Mr. Butler recognized that the best that could be hoped for was a federation with powers at the centre so watered down that it would in effect be no more than an economic association. He also recognized that Nyasaland's leaders were determined to secede but hoped that when their right to do so had been established, Nyasaland's weak economic position would encourage them to cooperate in building some sort of economic association with their neighbours. (This hope, too, proved abortive.) At the end of June 1962 Mr. Butler announced the names of a group of advisers who were to visit the Federal territories and examine for him the question of future relationships. Led by Sir Roger Stevens, then of the Foreign Office, the group consisted of Sir Ralph Hone, a constitutional expert, Professor Arthur Brown, Professor of Economics at Leeds University (where Sir Roger Stevens is now Vice-Chancellor) and Mr. D. A. Scott, who was deputy High Commissioner in Salisbury. Mr. Butler summarized their task as follows:

The advisers have as their first job the task of examining with the Nyasaland Government before any final conclusion is reached, the economic and financial consequences for Nyasaland of withdrawal from the Federation. They also have the task of examining possible and acceptable forms of association with the other territories, and also with the Governments of Northern and Southern Rhodesia possible forms in which all three territories might be associated or any alternative form which might be worked out.

Even Sir Roy Welensky and his colleagues were by now convinced that major changes were going to be necessary, though they maintained that the Federation could not simply be legislated out of existence. They seized on anything that might possibly strengthen their case, and in this context it is worth recalling one of Mr. Butler's rare blunders. On July 10, 1962, at a dinner of the Rhodesia and Nyasaland Club at the Savoy Hotel, he urged investors to have faith in the Federation.

We want you to understand that if you put your money into the Federation we shall be behind you . . . The economic potential of the Federation is outstanding and there is no reason at all–and I want to make this quite clear to you tonight who are engaged in business and industry and commerce–there is no reason at all why this economic potential should not develop if there can be orderly progress without strife and this is what we are out to achieve. Progress depends on political as well as economic development and here also the record of the Federation is a good one, whatever may have been said at the United Nations.

What Mr. Butler presumably intended was 'Invest in Central Africa'. His mistake was swiftly taken up by the Federal Government (and later his remarks were published in their White Paper).* They saw it as an indication that he had decided that the Federation should continue, whereas in fact at that time he had reached the conclusion that it could not in its present form, and was open-minded about the future type of association. In itself, the error was trivial. In the atmosphere of mistrust and suspicion that had grown up between the British and Federal Governments, it was important. Mr. Butler is a man whose utterances are often obscure, but in his dealings with the Federal Government he was more straightforward than any of his predecessors. He started with the disadvantage that normal contact had already broken down. It was all the more important, therefore, that equivocations should be replaced by plain-speaking, and still within the British Cabinet there seemed to be unwillingness to speak plainly to Sir Roy — though he for his part by this time never hesitated to say precisely and publicly what he thought about Mr. Macmillan and his colleagues.

The question of Nyasaland's secession was a case in point, As I have explained, it was by now accepted by the British Government that Nyasaland would secede. It was also obvious to – though not accepted by – Sir Roy Welensky. All that remained to settle was the form and timing of the announcement, and there was surely everything to be said for facing Sir Roy Welensky with the decision so that at least he would be able to express his views well in advance of the act, and would not be able to claim that it had been sprung upon him. By August 1962 Mr. Butler's hopes of creating a suc-cessor régime to the Federation were fading fast. He had by then decided not only that Nyasaland would have to be allowed to secede, but that the announcement of her right would have to be made during the visit to London of Dr. Banda, the Prime Minister, planned for November that year.

The announcement that the British Government accepted in

* *The Issue of Nyasaland's Secession,* C. Fed. 231.

I

principle the secession of Nyasaland from the Federation was made in the House of Commons on December 19, 1962. In a speech on that day to the Federal Assembly Sir Roy said:

My Government were informed only after the decision had been made by British Ministers. We were not consulted before the decision was reached. On Saturday, the 3rd November, I was informed that the British Government had decided that an announcement would be made before the commencement of the Nyasaland conference, due to start on the 12th November; and that the British Government had agreed in principle to the secession of that territory from the Federation. At my request this decision was reported to Federal Ministers by the British High Commissioner [Lord Alport] on Monday morning, the 5th November.

He added: 'We, as a government, were completely ignored and side-stepped.'

For tactical reasons the British Government decided to delay the announcement until after the Nyasaland conference, but this did not alter the justice of Sir Roy Welensky's claim that he had not been consulted. It is hard to find any good reason for not telling him earlier what was going to happen, and when, since the general outline of British Government thinking was no secret. Sir Roy records in *Welensky's 4,000 Days* that already in April Lord Alport had seen him to sketch out Mr. Butler's preliminary ideas, which included the suggestion that a committee should be set up to investigate whether Nyasaland should continue to be associated with the Rhodesias. Sir Roy Welensky opposed this suggestion—and as usual failed to produce any constructive alternative. He was in fact no help to Mr. Butler in his task, and the task being what it was, could hardly have been expected to be, but it was foolish to give him an opportunity to claim, with good reason, that the British Government had behaved improperly.

This he did, as we have already seen, at frequent intervals, but the most ferocious example was at the time of the Nyasaland secession announcement. In his speech to the Federal Assembly already referred to he quoted speeches by British Ministers over the years and pointed out how the pledges contained in them had been broken. This speech by Sir Roy and one that he made on the following day, December 20, 1962, were published by the Federal Government, together with statements made in the House of Lords on December 19 by Lord Salisbury, Lord Chandos, Lord

Boyd, Lord Colyton and Lord Malvern, who had all been concerned with the foundation of the Federation (Lord Malvern as its first Prime Minister, and before that, Prime Minister of Southern Rhodesia, and the others as British Ministers). Among the references made by Sir Roy Welensky were the following.

He quoted from the Report of the Conference on Federation held in London in January 1953 (Cmnd 8753) the passage which read:

To give the new Federal State time to establish itself, and to build up confidence in the Federation among all the peoples of the Territories, provision has been made that, for a period of ten years after the constitution comes into force, there shall be no change in the division of powers between the Federation and the territories except with the consent of all three territorial legislatures.

He quoted a statement by Lord Swinton (Secretary of State for Commonwealth Relations at the time) from the minutes of the conference in which he said:

I know no Federal constitution within the Commonwealth, or indeed I think outside it, in which a secession clause is to be found, and there must be very good reason for that . . . It would be right to describe a claim to secede as a precursor of liquidation . . . there is one absolutely overriding economic objection to this which rules it out from the very start. The Federation has got to raise (loans) on federal assets and federal securities. Make no mistake about it . . . Federation could never raise a penny of money by loan if it were not known whether Federation was to continue, and therefore whatever views you take about what I may call the moral side of the thing, there is an economic argument to which there can be no possible answer . . .

He referred to the intention in 1953 that 'any proposals to terminate the constitution could only be put into effect with the concurrence of the Federal Government and of the three territorial governments, and of Her Majesty's Government in the United Kingdom'. He quoted from statements in support of this intention by Lord Chandos (who, as Oliver Lyttleton, was the Colonial Secretary of the day) and Lord Swinton.

In the House of Lords on December 19 Lord Salisbury (who was Commonwealth Secretary in 1952) said:

We have been told this afternoon that Her Majesty's Government have decided unilaterally to agree in principle to the secession of Nyasaland from the Federation. That, my Lords, was the one thing which the

Conservative Government, at the time when the Federation was set up in 1953, pledged themselves not to do . . . I can assure your Lordships that there can be no doubt at all that British Ministers at the conference gave most explicit assurances that the constitution of the new Federation that was being set up would not be liquidated without the free assent of all the Governments concerned; and that included the Federal Government . . .

Lord Chandos said that if his memory was correct, as he thought it was, the pledges were given.

Lord Boyd (Minister of State for Colonial Affairs in 1951 and 1952 and later–1954 to 1959–Colonial Secretary) said:

In the following year I came back to the Colonial Office as Secretary of State and had some close associations with central Africa for five years. I, of course, knew of the undertakings about secession that had been given during the course of the various discussions, and I realized that these undertakings were regarded as pledges (as we ourselves regarded them) by the people to whom they were addressed. It was in the confidence engendered by these pledges that federation was born, that investment was encouraged, and that plans for a liberal and progressive policy in Central Africa were laid down.

Lord Colyton (who as Henry Hopkinson had been Minister of State for Colonial Affairs from 1952 to 1955) said: 'I was present throughout those meetings and I remember very well what was said. The British Government's representatives stated categorically that the federal constitution could not be liquidated or upset without the concurrence of all the governments involved.'

The breaking of these pledges and the statements made in the House of Lords drew widespread condemnation on the British Government from quarters which accepted the rightness of the secession decision as well as those which thought the Federation should be somehow kept in being. Mr. Butler certainly had a difficult decision to make. In 1962 it was quite clear that the Federation could not be kept in being, and that Nyasaland could not be forced to stay in it–except by military force. It was clear also that giving the pledges, even in the atmosphere prevailing in 1952 and 1953, was inept and irresponsible. Mr. Denis Healey, M.P., (Labour) indeed declared in the House of Commons on December 20, 1962, that making the pledges and concealing them from Parliament had been 'furtive and dishonourable', since their effect was to renounce Parliament's power of legislation.

Making them, in any case, would have been reasonable only if human opinions were unchangeable. The attitude to African affairs in 1953 is admirably reflected in Lord Swinton's remark that 'whatever views you take about what I may call the moral side of the thing, there is an economic argument to which there can be no possible answer'.

By the end of 1962, the British Government had been forced into recognizing that economic arguments are never unanswerable nor capable of withstanding a strong political tide.

In short, in announcing Nyasaland's right to secede, Mr. Butler was simply being realistic. Had the Cabinet decided to pursue a different policy, they would have been guilty of serious irresponsibility. The fault lay in the method. Every effort should have been made to get the Federal Government to accept the inevitable through discussion. The existence of the pledges should have been frankly acknowledged, and Sir Roy's cooperation sought in extricating the British Government from the unpleasant duty of breaking them. If he had refused, then at least the thing would have been played openly and honourably.

The breaking of the pledges gave Sir Roy Welensky the chance to recall other more recent examples of double-talk by British Ministers. He quoted from a speech by Mr. Macmillan, the Prime Minister, in Salisbury on January 19, 1960, in which he had said:

First I should like to make it plain that the function of the Monckton Commission is not to destroy the Federation – far from it. It is to advise us how the Federation can best go forward . . . May I quote words I have used in Parliament, especially in connection with the Monckton Commission. This is what I said on July 22nd immediately after the passage which I have just quoted:

'. . . If we were to announce our intention now to disband the Federation or form a new one, or to divide it into different units without waiting either for the Commission or for the 1960 review; if we were to tear up, without further thought, an experiment which is only seven years old and which was started with a great deal of good will on all sides, and an experiment which has made very considerable progress, we should be guilty of an act of treachery towards the high ideals and purposes which we set ourselves.'

I stand by these words – all of them – and I do not wish to add to them.

Sir Roy also quoted remarks made by Lord Home (then Secretary of State for Commonwealth Relations, later, as Sir Alec Douglas-Home, Prime Minister) at a press conference in Salisbury on February 26, 1960, when he said:

Now I have been asked many times since I have been here in the last ten days what is the British Government's attitude to Federation. Well, I will recall to you, if I may, the 1957 Declaration which we made and which will no doubt be fairly fresh in your minds, and I will read a part of it to you:

'Her Majesty's Government in the United Kingdom and the Government of the Federation of Rhodesia and Nyasaland have already made it clear and take this opportunity of reaffirming that they are opposed to any proposal either for the amalgamation into a unitary state of the territories now composing the Federation or for the secession of any one of those territories from the Federation.'

And I want to reaffirm that we believe in Federation and we want to see how it can best be made to work for the benefit of all its peoples and find a solution which will be acceptable to all its peoples, and that is our intention and so I hope there will be no doubt about that.

It was small wonder that Sir Roy felt bitter, and even his own unconstructive attitude does not excuse behaviour which convicts the British Government of thorough-going dishonesty–unless one assumes that British ministers were so stupid that they could not see what was happening.

Mr. Butler, in taking over responsibility for Central Africa, inherited a morass. He had to dismember a Federal Government that not only had been brought to birth by the British Government itself, but which had a strong instinct for self-preservation. To do this, he had international responsibility but virtually no power, and certainly no physical manifestation of power. One of the greatest difficulties in British dealings with the Federation, and, after its demise, with Southern Rhodesia, has been the fact that no British soldier or civil servant worked there. The administration was local; so was the defence framework. Mr. Butler, faced with the sort of mess that no competent government would have allowed to develop, had to do everything by diplomacy. His mastery of political method, his keen brain and his addiction to barely comprehensible nuances all helped him to succeed in one of the most complicated jobs of his political career.

That he did succeed was proved at the end of 1963 when, on December 31, according to plan, the Federation ceased to exist. I toured the three territories just before the end of the year, and found that people were accepting the inevitable now that it was upon them with remarkably little fuss. Even Sir Roy Welensky, presiding over a government with nothing more to do than settle the final funeral arrangements of a country which no longer had any reality, had ceased to be the doughty fighter ready to 'go the whole hog' or take on the British Cabinet single-handed.

The year from the announcement of Nyasaland's right to secede to the end of the Federation was not all plain sailing. There were several occasions when Mr. Butler was faced with a breakdown in discussions on the highly complicated arrangements that had to be made. Taking a three-part Federation to pieces is, if anything, more complicated than putting it together, because assets and liabilities, civil servants and soldiers, communications and currencies, have to be shared out or replaced. Accusations of perfidious behaviour continued to be made by Sir Roy Welensky and his colleagues, particularly when Mr. Butler announced (on April 1, 1963) that the right of secession was accepted also in the case of Northern and Southern Rhodesia. The mechanics of dissolution were discussed at a conference at Victoria Falls (appropriately enough, that was where the Federation was conceived) in June and July 1963, and one of Mr. Butler's major triumphs was persuading all concerned to take part. Southern Rhodesia, whose Prime Minister then was Mr. Winston Field, at first refused to play any part in the Victoria Falls discussions unless she first was granted independence. She was moved from that position to agreeing to attend the conference by a remarkable series of letters from Mr. Butler, in which Mr. Field was gradually weaned away from his rigid first stand. The exchange of letters was published as a White Paper.*

Just over ten years after it was launched, therefore, the Federation of Rhodesia and Nyasaland came to an inglorious end. Its conception was unwise and ill-prepared. It was imposed against popular feeling. Successive Conservative British Governments failed to press the Federal Government to adopt more realistic, and more popular, policies. Instead, they permitted more and

* *Correspondence between Her Majesty's Government and the Government of Southern Rhodesia, April–June, 1963.* Cmnd 2073.

more power to rest in the hands of the authorities in Salisbury, less and less in Whitehall. Finally, having belatedly recognized that break-up was inevitable, they consistently failed to deal honestly with the obsolescent Federal Government.

Chapter 10

More Federal Follies

I HAVE written at length about the Federation of Rhodesia and Nyasaland because it is a classic case of colonial failure and one that is fresh in many people's memories. It is also, incidentally, one that aroused intense political controversy in Africa, in Britain and in the United Nations. As I have tried to shew, the Rhodesian Federation was doomed to failure from the beginning, and its failure was clearly apparent to most intelligent observers by the end of 1960 at the latest. In spite of this Central African object lesson so constantly and tiresomely before them, and in spite of the similarly telling lesson of the West Indies Federation, which disintegrated and which the British Government brought formally to an end in May 1962, the Conservative Government was obsessed with the federal concept and kept on creating federations in a positive frenzy. They have proved to be depressingly ramshackle edifices. When I was planning this chapter, I had determined to discuss the difficulties involved in making federations work. Just before I was ready to write it, Singapore parted from its federal partners in Malaysia and the plans for constitutional progress in South Arabia had to be put into cold storage because of tensions within that unstable union—two graphic illustrations of what I wanted to say.

Working a federation is far more difficult than working a unitary state. It requires a large measure of tolerance between different and potentially rival governments, each jealous of its own exclusive powers. It requires agreement on a good working relationship between politicians at the centre and in the constituent parts. It requires good communications and, ideally, a homogeneous society, and a coincidence of economic aims. It is highly desirable that the federation should come into being spontaneously. These criteria for success can be deduced, it seems to me, from an examination of actual federations and their record. Even those which have survived successfully for many years provide evidence from time to

133

time of the severe strains and stresses which are inherent in the system. The United States, for example, still faces controversy over states' rights versus federal authority, particularly in such things as the political integration of Negroes. Canada has recently seen a serious crisis in Quebec, where a racial and cultural minority has resented domination by the English-speaking majority.

Applying my list of criteria for success to federal creations of British colonial policy produces an interesting pattern.

TOLERANCE BETWEEN GOVERNMENTS

This was absent in Central Africa, where the United Federal Party at the centre spoke with a totally different voice from the Colonial Office, the effective power in Northern Rhodesia and Nyasaland. Between the UFP and the various African nationalist parties–the men on the threshold of governmental power–there was, of course, total opposition.

It was absent in the West Indies, where there was constant discord between the Federal Government and the units, particularly over freedom of movement of individuals between the constituent parts of the Federation, and fiscal and financial control, including the right to levy taxes.

There was a lack of tolerance between the centre and Singapore in the Malaysia Federation which increased to the point where an accommodation was no longer possible. Similarly there has from the beginning been mistrust between the other constituents, Sarawak and Sabah, and the centre, based on fears of Malay domination of the administration.

In South Arabia, Aden, as the most constitutionally and economically advanced of the federal constituents, had to be given special constitutional safeguards against the Federal Government.

The countries of East Africa–Tanzania, Kenya and Uganda–though paying lip service to the desirability of federation, proved incapable of introducing it, since they failed to see eye to eye on a whole range of important issues, economic and political.

THE RELATIONSHIP BETWEEN POLITICIANS

The importance of this can be seen in the West Indies, where, significantly, the most able and dynamic of the political leaders–Dr. Eric Williams of Trinidad and Tobago and Mr. Norman Manley of Jamaica (later defeated by Sir Alexander Bustamante)–

preferred to remain in island politics. Between them and the Federal Government led by Sir Grantley Adams there was a relationship which ranged from cool to frigid.

In central Africa the Federal leaders not only refused to recognize the importance of the up and coming African leaders, but in most cases had scarcely met them. Sir Roy Welensky and Mr. Kenneth Kaunda, for example, had their nearest approach to a friendly encounter at Chequers at a time when they were engaged in bitter combat over constitutional matters. The harsh words that were uttered so frequently by the protagonists in the Central African drama about each other were certainly made harsher by the fact that they were grounded in mutual ignorance.

One of the causes of discord in Malaysia was a breakdown between Tunku Abdul Rahman and Mr. Lee Kuan Yew, two men of widely different character, background and type of intellect.

In South Arabia the most obvious weakness of the federal idea was that it attempted a marriage between politicians who were relatively progressive in Aden (and who were anyway likely to be replaced by even more dedicated 'progressives' backed by the forces of Arab nationalism) and largely feudal rulers in the Aden protectorate states.

Part of the failure to federate in East Africa must be attributed to personal jealousies between the national leaders, particularly since any arrangement which put Mr. Kenyatta at the top (a position he would certainly get through age and prestige) and Mr. Nyerere in second place (which *he* would have earned by seniority and because he was the inspirer of East African federation), would leave Mr. Obote of Uganda out in the cold.

GOOD COMMUNICATIONS AND A HOMOGENEOUS SOCIETY

The islands of the West Indies lie hundreds of miles apart (Jamaica is 1,000 miles from Trinidad), and apart from politicians and a few other special cases, people travel little between them. Cost, if nothing else, ensures this.

Communications between the constituents of Malaysia also are not good, certainly at the level of the ordinary population. There, too, racial differences mean that society is far from homogeneous. There is a fundamental potential discord between the Malays, who dominate politically, and the Chinese, who are generally better educated, more energetic and dominant in trade and commerce. As I have already mentioned, the non-Malay people of Sabah and Sarawak tend to resent domination by Malays.

Racial differences were the cardinal problem in the Federation of Rhodesia and Nyasaland, where all the talk of partnership and multi-racialism could not conceal that a racial minority had, and intended to retain, political power.

In Nigeria, one of the main causes of discord and dissension between the regions and within the Federal Government coalition was ill feeling, not between black and white, but between the various peoples of the Federation and in particular between the northerners and the people of the southern regions (principally the Ibo and the Yoruba). Removing these tribal animosities is one of the main problems facing the new military rulers of the country. Then, to take the case of a federation that has not come into existence, relations between Senegal and The Gambia stopped well short of political union largely because although their peoples are tribally linked and the two countries make a geographical whole, their ways of thought and methods of administration are totally different. Even discussions on functional links were hampered by the lack of communication inherent in Senegal's Frenchness and The Gambia's Englishness.

ECONOMIC AIMS

Relative economic strengths and weaknesses can easily create jealousies, or heighten those caused by other factors. In Central Africa, although economic issues were obviously not crucial to the failure of the federation, there was much mutual resentment because of the poverty of Nyasaland (and the feeling that it was being carried by the other partners) and the mineral wealth of Northern Rhodesia, which always felt that it was being bled by Southern Rhodesia, the political centre of the Federation. Specific controversial issues arose from time to time such as, for example, the question whether to introduce the Kariba hydro-electric scheme or to choose an alternative in Northern Rhodesia, at Kafue.

Economic issues were of great importance in the West Indies where, as we have seen above, they were one of the main causes of friction between the central and island governments, and incidentally between the large and the small islands. Basically, Trinidad and Tobago and Jamaica, the largest units, were unwilling to carry economically the smaller islands at least unless they were able to dominate the Federation to a far greater extent than the constitution permitted.

In South Arabia, Aden is economically as well as constitutionally more advanced than the protectorate states, and has always been unwilling to subsidize them. The British Government was obliged to provide a heavy subvention (for the Federal army, for example) and in effect to meet the Federal budget.

With the three East African territories, linked in the East African Common Services Organization, economic rivalry has been of great importance. After political federation had proved to be impossible, economic jealousies increased. Uganda, being landlocked, has always been suspicious of its neighbours, fearing that they will use their geographical advantage to coerce her. Kenya, whose capital Nairobi is the commercial capital of the region, and which was developed far more actively during colonial days, has naturally been resented by the other two. Tanzania in particular, a poor country, and the first of the three to become independent, has resented the fact that investors tend to prefer Kenya.

SPONTANEITY

Strictly speaking, none of the territories we are considering has come to federal status as the result of a popular movement. Nigeria, the most successful federation among the newer countries, was united by the colonial rulers. The fact that, as one country, Nigeria can play a far more significant role internationally than as three or four separate states has encouraged the country's leaders to accept a continuing marriage.

One of the worst examples of a non-spontaneous federation was Rhodesia and Nyasaland, as we have seen in a previous chapter. The marriage of Aden and the protectorate states in the Federation of South Arabia had all the signs of a shot-gun wedding, with the British Government firing the gun. In Malaysia, too, the doubts, or at best the apathy, of the people, particularly in Sarawak and Sabah, were submerged in a constitutional hustle. It is not without significance that the constitutional agreement to bring Malaysia into being was signed, after a long series of wrangles and a good deal of forceful talk by Mr. Duncan Sandys, in the middle of the night—hardly a time to choose if negotiations had gone smoothly. Even in the West Indies, where there was a long-standing desire by leaders to forge closer links, the actual impetus to federation came in a despatch from the late Colonel Oliver Stanley, then Colonial Secretary, to the West Indies governments in March 1945, in which he stressed that

the aim of British policy should be the development of federation in the Caribbean at such times as the balance of opinion in the various colonies is in favour of a change and when the development of communications makes it administratively practicable. The ultimate aim of any federation which may be established would be full internal self-government within the British Commonwealth.

The idea of a political federation was debated by the colonial legislatures in the West Indies at Stanley's suggestion.

Although the experience of other colonial powers is outside the scope of this book, it is worth remarking that they have been no more successful than Britain in producing federations. France's dream of her West African and Equatorial African possessions continuing as federations closely linked with metropolitan France remained a dream, and the territories eventually followed the example of Guinea (which chose independence in 1958) and became separately independent in 1960.

The Federation of the West Indies came into being in January 1958. Apart from Jamaica and Trinidad and Tobago, it included Barbados, the Windward Islands (Grenada, Dominica, St. Lucia, St. Vincent) and the Leeward Islands (Antigua, Montserrat and St. Christopher, Nevis and Anguilla). The Federal capital was in Trinidad. The moves towards federation had taken place over a number of years, and the idea of federation was broadly accepted at a conference at Montego Bay, Jamaica, in 1947. In 1948 and 1949 the Standing Closer Association Committee under Sir Hubert Rance drafted a report, recommending a two-chamber legislature and a system of government on Australian lines, which was basically that eventually introduced. In 1953 – the year in which the Rhodesia and Nyasaland Federation was launched – a London conference agreed on a *Plan for a British Caribbean Federation* (Cmnd 8895, 1953) and two years later this plan had been adopted by the West Indies legislatures. After further discussion and examination of particular aspects of federation, a final conference took place in London early in 1956 and the West Indies agreed to be 'bound

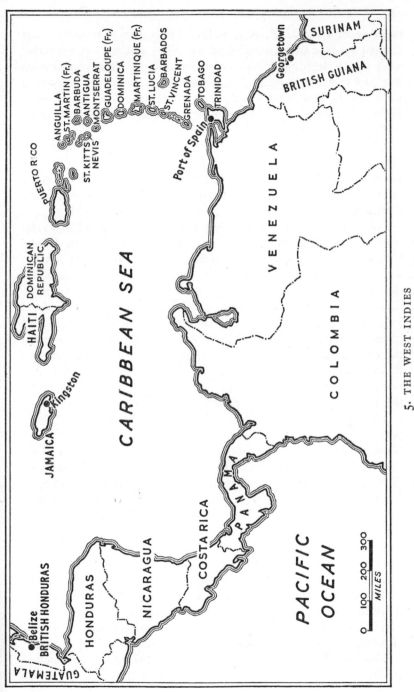

5. THE WEST INDIES

On independence in May 1966 British Guiana became Guyana

together in federation'. A Standing Federation Committee was formed to make administrative preparations and carry out detailed work on the drafting of the constitution. The Federal constitution was promulgated as an Order in Council in July 1957. Elections were held in March 1958 and brought to power The West Indies Federal Labour Party. Princess Margaret inaugurated the Federal Parliament on April 22, 1958.

There had thus been more than ten years of active preparation before the federation became a reality, but it lasted for barely four years and on February 6, 1962, following Jamaica's decision by referendum to secede, the Colonial Secretary announced that the British Government were arranging for it to be dissolved.

For part of the cause of failure it is necessary only to look at the constitution. In many respects this was a standard federal constitution, but the Federal Government suffered from one notable weakness. It was not empowered to levy income tax, and its main source of revenue was an annual levy on territorial governments based on hypothetical customs and excise duties. The Federal Legislature had the right to make laws with regard to customs and excise duties but the Federal Government was permitted to retain the revenue from such duties only on certain scheduled commodities. Furthermore, there was an upper limit during the first five years on the Federal revenue to be obtained in this way. In short, the Federal Government was hamstrung.

The weaknesses had been noted and commented on over a long period. British newspapers, notably *The Times* and *The Manchester Guardian* (as it then was), underlined the doubts among the West Indians themselves in articles in 1953. The economic dependence of the area on Great Britain—and the fact that Britain would therefore be bound to exercise a measure of economic and financial control—were discussed. Numerous reports indicated both the existence of hostility to the Federal idea in some quarters, and the fact that although there was widespread agreement on the principle there were great differences on the details. The fact that enthusiasm was greater in the smaller islands—which had more to gain—than in Jamaica, Trinidad and Barbados, was duly recorded. After the 1956 conference *The Times* emphasized in an editorial Mr. Lennox-Boyd's observation that the powers of the Federal Government as proposed appeared to be rather weak.

This was the position when a constitutional conference opened in London at the end of May 1961. Its avowed purpose was to fix an independence date and agree an independence constitution for the West Indies—and in fact it did so. The date chosen was May 31, 1962, the day on which, in melancholy fact, the federation was dissolved. The issues outstanding when the conference began were absolutely crucial in spite of preliminary meetings in the West Indies. The argument between the supporters of a strong central government and the supporters of a system in which most power would reside in the units continued. Trinidad belonged to the first group, Jamaica to the second. The smaller islands feared domination by the larger, and particularly by Jamaica. The principle of freedom of movement between the territories was accepted, but in practice, limitations were to remain. The method of financing the Federal Government was still unsatisfactory, and by the time the delegates met in Lancaster House under the chairmanship of Mr. Iain Macleod it was clear that the larger islands' readiness to leave Federal posts to the small island men (the Prime Minister, Sir Grantley Adams, comes from Barbados) was not accompanied by an equal readiness to give up power to them.

At the opening session Mr. Macleod accepted, in his speech, that the criteria considered necessary for nationhood included an adequate defence force, a diplomatic service, adequate central administration with adequate financial resources, central control of the currency, a customs union and freedom of movement of persons. He agreed that the difficulty of achieving these objectives might 'make it necessary to move forward in some of these fields at a deliberate speed and over a period of years'. He emphasized that the British Government did not intend to impose its views. Ironically, the public opening proceedings lasted two days, since all the premiers and chief ministers wished to speak.

Fears of Jamaican domination were reciprocated by Jamaican unwillingness to allow her industrial development to be controlled by representatives of the smaller islands. Mr. Norman Manley, the Premier of Jamaica, was unable to agree that Jamaica should give up her effective veto on the removal of items from the reserve legislative list by accepting anything less than the decision of representatives of two-thirds of the Federal population. The only alternative he would accept was a formula based on unanimity of decision (which would, of course, give every island a veto). Trinidad shared the misgivings which other islands felt at the Jamaican formula, but Dr. Eric Williams, the Trinidad Premier, urged that it should be accepted, on the ground that if it was not, Jamaica would leave the Federation which would then be worthless.

After three weeks, the conference ended, but not in agreement. For one thing, the conference decisions were subject to approval by the separate legislatures, and in the case of Jamaica, by a referendum of the people, promised by Mr. Manley. He himself said there had been much more disagreement at the conference than he had expected. Dr. Williams, always a shrewd and perceptive analyst, was extremely gloomy, particularly on the question of freedom of movement. This, as he pointed out, was the one important economic matter left in Federal Government hands. Industrial development and income tax, on the other hand, were subject to the veto of any island (against Trinidad's wishes) but Trinidad could accept that only if freedom of movement were also left in unit hands. In an interview with me on June 19, 1961, Dr. Williams foresaw three events which could wreck the Federation: a decision by Jamaica to leave (this is in fact what happened); a decision by any of the small islands to insist on immediate freedom of movement; or, finally, whatever the others did, a decision by Trinidad not to accept a situation in which the one issue–freedom of movement–vitally affecting Trinidad was the one left in Federal hands.

The report of the conference (Cmnd 1417) included the framework for the independence constitution and named May 31, 1962, as independence day. It was quite obvious, however, that the framework shewed signs, even before it was published, of coming apart at the seams. The problem of power had not been solved. The Federation in its new constitutional garb would be clothed in all the same old weaknesses. The politicians who were attracted to the centre, like the powers that they enjoyed there, would in all probability continue to be the second-liners. One of the most impressive West Indies political leaders, discussing the situation with me, remarked unkindly but with an element of justification that by its past showing the Federal Government was not a weak or bad government–it was a vacuum. Whether the criticisms of the Federal Government were justified or greatly exaggerated by personal antagonisms and jealousies, the important fact was that unless the most able men were attracted to the centre, central authority would not be taken seriously or accepted by Jamaica or Trinidad who must necessarily in practice dominate the Federation for years ahead. Since Dr. Williams had no intention of leaving Trinidad politics for federal, this meant that Mr. Manley would have to be ready to become Federal Prime Minister. Mr. Manley himself recognized this, and would probably have been willing, if reluctant, to accept the challenge, but before the question could arise his own voters, in exercising the democratic right which he felt was properly theirs, had withdrawn Jamaica from the Federation (and were soon to remove him from power in an election which put in office once more Sir Alexander Bustamante).

With its record of policy disagreements and ineffective central control, the Federation was clearly not a healthy infant. The 1961 conference was the opportunity to strengthen it, and the British Government could reasonably have played a more active part in this process, by exhortation and direction, and also by a more imaginative attitude to the economic ills of the area. Historically, after all, Britain owed much to the West Indies, and the economic weaknesses could—and still can—be fairly blamed on years of inattention. What is more, the constitutional maturity of even the smaller islands, their fitness to practise democracy on their own, was far greater than that of many African territories which were launched far more readily. It is hard to confute the opinion of Dr. Eric Williams (which I last heard him express in London in July 1965) that Britain has had no policy for the Caribbean for thirty or forty years.

Whatever their attitude previously, the Colonial Office was certainly capable of reading the ominous warnings of the 1961 conference. For all the brave words about independence, for all the talk about providing the West Indies with 'its opportunity to plan an effective and constructive role in international affairs' the conference report was a blueprint for failure.

Yet when Jamaica's referendum brought matters dramatically to a head, the seriousness of the resulting situation seemed to take Whitehall by surprise. Though continuing to support the Federation, the British Government had not been willing to use their opportunity, through economic pressure, to try and strengthen the Federal administration. Nor, however, had they worked out the likely consequences of this unwillingness. Other problems in other areas had proved to be more pressing.

Jamaica made its decision in September 1961. At the end of the month the Colonial Office announced that a further conference would be necessary 'to consider constitutional questions affecting the Federation arising from Jamaica's expressed desire to leave it'. It was realized by responsible people, and certainly by Sir Grantley Adams, that once Jamaica had decided to leave, Trinidad was most unlikely to agree to remain. Economically, after all, Trinidad was better placed for independence than Jamaica. At the end of September and the beginning of October 1961 Sir Grantley Adams was in London for talks at the Colonial Office (at the end of which the announcement about a further conference was made). On the assumption that Trinidad would follow Jamaica out, he was then thinking in terms of a Federal grouping of Barbados and the seven smaller islands. In other words, in spite of his own bitter disappointment, Sir Grantley Adams was at this moment taking an entirely realistic line.

In January 1962 Mr. Reginald Maudling, as Colonial Secretary, visited the West Indies to see for himself what had to be done. Soon after his return he announced to the House of Commons (on February 8, 1962) that the Government had decided

to introduce legislation into Parliament very shortly which will enable us to dissolve the present Federation, and to set up an interim organization under a Commissioner appointed by Her Majesty's Government, which will be responsible for running the common services for the time being, until some more permanent arrangements for their operation can be worked out in conjunction with the Governments of the West Indies.

He explained that this decision had been taken in the light of agreement by the Premier of Barbados and the chief ministers of the Leeward and Windward Islands that the existing Federation should be dissolved, and that a new one should be created. This suggestion Mr. Maudling described as helpful but remarked that the Government considered 'that a great deal of careful study both here and in the West Indies will be needed before any final decisions can be taken . . .'

One aspect of the British Government's hasty acceptance of the inevitable, and their urgent plans for speedy burial of the Federal corpse, was that they acted without properly consulting the Federal Government which was still, as Sir Grantley said, 'the democratically elected organ of the people of the whole area'. He released to the press a letter which he wrote to Mr. Maudling on March 12, 1962, describing the procedure which the British Government were adopting as arbitrary and hurried and contrary to the spirit of the Federal Constitution. It completely alters the character of the relationship that should exist between Her Majesty's Government and the Federal Government, which was established in order to inherit full responsibility for the peace, good government and order of the territories which agreed to federate at Lancaster House on the 23rd of February, 1956.

Sir Grantley described the British legislation as 'a retrograde step in the history of the West Indies' and said parts of it negated 'the principle of responsible or even representative government which The West Indies have hitherto assumed was accepted by Her Majesty's Government'.

Mr. Maudling acted as he did because the Federal legislature was preparing to take action to provide payments in compensation for loss of office to Ministers and M.P.s as well as civil servants, and the British Government felt that the sum was excessive. As Britain would have to foot the bill, some action was obviously justified, but the procedure adopted was clumsy. Having failed to lead and persuade the Federation into success, which would have been at least worth trying, the British Government ignored completely the highly developed sense of constitutional propriety which marks the West Indies islands out as mature exponents of a British style of democracy.

Both Jamaica and Trinidad with Tobago became fully independent states within a few days of each other in August 1962. The future of the smaller islands following the failure of the Federation, however, was and remains bleak. A conference on the possibility of a new Federation of the East Caribbean (usually known as the 'Little Eight') took place in May 1962. It reached agreement in principle and produced an outline for a federal constitution (Cmnd 1746) but as the speeches at the public opening session suggested, agreement in principle was not the same as agreement in practice. Bitterness at Britain's attitude to the old Federation was one of the main themes of these speeches. Another was the insistence that in any federation the individual islands must retain their ministerial trappings, however much lip service might be paid to strength at the centre–and however absurd it might be to have a Chief Minister in charge of a government resembling an urban district council.

A year later, another conference to take the matter further was postponed. In the meantime Grenada, under a new government, had dropped out. The Little Eight became the Little Seven. Early in 1964 there was a further delay. When it finally took place, the meeting had little purpose, and by the middle of 1965 the hopes for a new West Indies Federation had vanished, to be replaced by a new constitutional experiment, under which the Leeward and Windward Islands will enjoy autonomy, under a British umbrella, with the right at any time to demand complete independence.

Chapter II

South Arabia and Malaysia

IN July 1961, when the British Government was dithering between irreconcilable aims in Northern Rhodesia, and when the Federation of Rhodesia and Nyasaland was beginning to look extremely unhealthy, talks took place in London on the future of Aden Colony and Protectorate. At these talks ministers of the Federal Supreme Council–that is of the federation formed by the states of the western Aden Protectorate–and ministers from the Colony of Aden, agreed to hold further discussions on the establishment of much closer links between the Federation and the Colony.

Towards the end of 1961, when Jamaica had decided to leave the West Indies Federation and Sir Grantley Adams was discussing with British ministers what was to be done with the remaining islands, Tunku Abdul Rahman, the Prime Minister of Malaya, held talks with the British Government about the possibility of creating the Federation of Malaysia, to include Singapore, North Borneo, Sarawak and Brunei (which never, in fact, joined Malaysia).

By March 1962, the Rhodesia and Nyasaland Federation had received the death blow implicit in the Northern Rhodesia constitution. The West Indies Federation had been placed in commission by the British Government and a date fixed for its formal dismantling. Five months later, in August 1962, agreement on the creation of Malaysia was announced. In the same month, a White Paper was published (Cmnd 1814) setting out details of the proposed accession of Aden to the Federation of South Arabia (as the western protectorate grouping had by then been named).

The failure of two federations did not discourage the British Government from backing two new ones. Indeed, death and conception were virtually simultaneous. British enthusiasm for federations, however, was not an adequate substitute for proper planning and preparation and an examination of developments in South Arabia and Malaysia reveals serious gaps in the plans, and even more in the policies pursued by Whitehall.

147

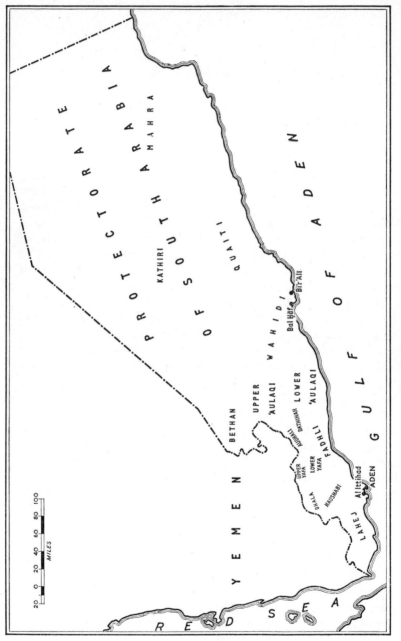

6. SOUTH ARABIA

In 1961 the leaders of the Federation of Arab Amirates of the South (as South Arabia was called) were due to meet in London to discuss administrative and constitutional matters, and in particular, questions of British financial aid. At that time there were already murmurings of a wider grouping, which would draw in Aden Colony. Mr. Macleod, as Colonial Secretary, invited ministers from the Colony to London to take part in the talks, which ended early in July with the issue of a communiqué announcing that it had been agreed that further discussions should take place with a view to the establishment of a much closer link between the existing Federation and the Colony. These further talks were held in Aden under the chairmanship of the Governor, Sir Charles Johnston. They began in August, and were informal. In January 1962 the Governor made a statement which, he emphasized, was made with the authority of the British Government. It read:

Her Majesty's Government consider that there are great advantages for both Colony and Federation in a much closer link between them. It is our policy to bring them together. The best method of achieving that purpose forms the subject of the current discussions in Aden. These talks are making reasonable progress, considering the complexity of the constitutional, administrative and financial problems involved. All those who were taking part in them earnestly wish that they will result in agreed proposals which, as has already been promised, will then be made public and put before this Council the Aden legislature and before the Federal Council for discussions. The desirability in principle of such a link is however already clear, and it follows that constitutional advance in Aden Colony must be designed to facilitate this link. Constitutional advance in the Colony will be considered in the near future during the current talks, and proposals on it will likewise be made public and put before this Council for consideration. When considering the proposals on all these matters which we hope will emerge, Her Majesty's Government will give full weight to the views expressed by this council and all others concerned.

As this statement makes quite plain, the discussions were a piece of window-dressing. With luck, they might produce some sort of consensus in favour of links, but whether they did or not, the British Government had decided that the links would be forged. The essential decision was pre-empted–'the desirability in principle of such a link is however already clear'–and the Governor's statement was an indication that however complex the problems might be, their complexity would not be permitted in the long run to hinder the creation of the new Federation.

Many criticisms have been levelled against the marriage of Aden and the protectorate states on the ground that it was a forced union of progress with feudalism. There is a good deal in this, particularly when one looks at the character of the original Federation – the protectorate states without Aden. The Supreme Council of Ministers of the Federation were the rulers of the states or their nominees. With the British Government there was a treaty of friendship and protection, under which Britain retained full control of defence and external affairs, and undertook to provide advice and financial and technical aid. British advice in any matter connected with the good government of the Federation was mandatory. The treaty with the Federation, however, did not supersede the separate treaties with the individual member states.

The Federation, in other words, was a club of autocratic rulers, whose nationhood was circumscribed not only by the limitations on sovereignty implicit, and explicit, in the treaty of protection, but also by the individuality of the separate states.

Aden had a measure of self-government under the 1959 constitution, but it certainly did not satisfy the Arab nationalists, whose most militant manifestation in the Colony was the Aden TUC. The Aden Government – or rather, its local element – was composed largely of moderate-minded businessmen rather than dynamic politicians, and not surprisingly it did not reflect adequately these Arab nationalist views.

In addition to the basic conflict of interests between the Colony and the Protectorate, there was within the Colony itself a substantial body of opposition to union, which could expect to find support among the large body of immigrant Yemeni workers in Aden. For this reason, the British authorities in looking forward to the election that was to fall due in Aden, in January 1963, began even in the autumn of 1961, just after the informal talks on links had begun, to think of postponing these elections so that the franchise could be changed in such a way that the immigrant Yemenis would be prevented from voting.

It did not take much prescience to see that the Arab nationalists represented the future whereas the feudal rulers were a relic of the past – a powerful relic, it is true, and one that would not quickly be changed in a territory as unsophisticated as South Arabia, but hardly an attractive cause for a colonial country with a policy and record of rapid devolution of power to back. Nor did it require much political acumen to see that limiting the franchise, and excluding from it a large and significant element of the population, was a policy fraught with dangers. The British Government lacked the limited prescience and acumen required.

In July and August 1962, ministers from both Colony and Protectorate gathered in London for a constitutional conference. It lasted for about a month, and its deliberations were marred by mutual mistrust between the Colony and the Protectorate representatives that had been growing during the months of consideration of the proposed union. By this time, Mr. Sandys had taken over the portfolio of the Colonies as well as that of Commonwealth Relations, and he was busy not only with the Aden talks but with those on Malaysia as well. With a typical display of stamina, he kept delegates working until the small hours in his efforts to bring them to agreement—though whether this system of midnight midwifery provides ideal, or even acceptable, conditions for the birth of new nations is in my view extremely doubtful.

On August 16, 1962, agreement was reached on proposals under which Aden would enter the Federation. The occasion was marked by an exchange of letters between Federal and Aden Ministers and the Colonial Secretary, published as a White Paper (Cmnd 1814). For their part, the ministers noted their conviction that the ending of the 'unnatural division' between Aden and the Federation, which was 'due to the accident of history, would be in the true interests of all who live in this area, and would contribute greatly to their prosperity and safety'. They accepted that Aden Colony should have special treatment, including larger representation proportionately than the existing member states of the Federation, because of her political and social institutions, which differed from those of the other states. They accepted, also, that Britain's sovereignty over Aden and in particular the bases there, should not be affected.

The British Government, apart from promising increased money to both Aden and the Federation to meet the additional costs of the union, undertook to conclude a treaty with the Federation in the terms proposed 'subject to approval by Parliament and by the Legislatures of the Federation and of Aden'. The terms included the proviso that Aden should accede to the Federation on March 1, 1963, or earlier.

The agreements included one most dubious provision, namely that the constitution of Aden should be amended so as to extend the maximum term of the Legislative Council from four to five years. This meant that it would not be necessary to hold an election in Aden before the union had been accomplished, and that therefore the decision on the merger would be taken by a legislature by no means representative of popular feeling in Aden. One has only to look at the political complexion and attitudes of the Aden Government in 1965, after an election had replaced the 'moderates' by a far more militant group, to appreciate the significance of this extension of the legislature's life. The main argument adduced in its favour, that it would permit the franchise revision to take place before the election, was not very convincing, and it became less and less so as the Aden Government's proposals for franchise revision emerged (some two years or more later) and were seen to involve not an extension but a limitation of voting rights. The decision to ignore the constitution and extend the life of the legislature by Order in Council, to put it bluntly, was a piece of gerrymandering on the part of the British Government to force through a constitutional change for which local support would not be forthcoming if events took their normal course.

By October 1962 the merger proposals had been approved by the two legislatures, but almost immediately an uprising had occurred in the Yemen against the traditional ruler–an uprising backed by Egypt, and sympathetically regarded by many residents in Aden, who thought of the South Arabian Federation as 'the occupied South Yemen'. A number of Aden ministers, who suffered from serious–and fully justified–doubts about the strength of their own political position, began to be less and less enthusiastic about a project which they could foresee bringing them personally nothing but trouble. The doubts were epitomized in the person of Muhammad Said Husseiny, one of the Aden Ministers, who in November 1962, after a long period of hesitation and several meetings with Mr. Duncan Sandys, decided to resign from the Aden Government. He had tried to persuade Mr. Sandys that, in the light of the Yemen uprising, the merger should be postponed so that elections could be held first in Aden. As soon as Mr. Sandys had announced in the House of Commons that the merger would go ahead as planned, Mr. Husseiny submitted his resignation. I saw him several times during this period, and it was quite clear that his resignation was not a hasty move but had been carefully thought out. Emphasizing as it did the shaky foundations on which the new Federation was being built, Mr. Husseiny's departure was a blow to the British Government. Mr. Sandys attempted to soften its effect by writing (and publishing) a letter to Mr. Husseiny which contained the following paragraph: 'In view of what you have told me of the intimidation and other pressures to which you have been subjected by opponents of the merger plan, I have no option but to accept your resignation with deep regret on behalf of the Governor.'

That 'intimidation and other pressures' were rife in Aden no one doubted. The implication of Mr. Sandys' letter, however, was that these pressures came from a small and unimportant minority, whereas in fact it was by now quite clear that popular feeling was against the merger. As an elected Minister, Mr. Husseiny was surely justified in demanding an election to test the people's will, and was not, in doing so, automatically proving himself a victim of intimidation. Not surprisingly he countered with a letter to Mr. Sandys in which he wrote:

I should like to emphasize very strongly that my resignation was not due to threats but to my conviction of imminent danger to general interests if the British Government were to insist on rushing the merger plan. I could easily have insisted on resigning much earlier and that I refrained to do so was due to the hope you would see the necessity for rethinking in the light of the ever-fermenting situation in the South and to the wish not to embarrass you or the Government while decisions were being taken.

My advice to you was to wait and watch events in the South with more patience than the British Government has shown. True negotiations have been spread over a long period but any one who has a real understanding of Arabs knows that there can never be too much. I feel that coercive policies like the one which you are now undertaking can result in grave danger not only to Britain and the free world but to the Arabs themselves. The federation and merger plans have often been presented as steps to Arab unity, but I have pointed out to you that to disassociate or separate any of the people of the South, whether in the Colony or the Protectorate or the Yemen is practically impossible. More especially when a foreign power is responsible for it. This is as true of the British as it was of the Egyptians or Turks in old days. Whether

Arabs are up-to-date citizens of Aden, Bedouins in the Protectorate or Yemeni tribes, they have their common Arabism.

The policy, therefore, of rushing things without proper consideration of the developments we are witnessing can only make enemies for Britain and leave the Arabs more divided than ever. In fact we think events have shown us that Arabs must be left to arrange their own future.

I have no pretensions to being an Arab expert, but it seems to me that the warning which Mr. Husseiny here gave has been amply justified by events. Even to a non-expert observer at the time, the indecent haste with which the merger plans were confirmed, the refusal to countenance any appeal to the Aden electorate, the insistence on putting all opposition down to terrorists and intimidators, smacked of the most foolish colonial steamroller tactics. It caused a good deal of heart-searching among officials and Government supporters. It certainly must have posed a delicate problem of conflicting loyalties to Mr. Nigel Fisher, who as Parliamentary Under-Secretary at the Colonial Office naturally had to support the official line, in spite of his own well-known 'liberalism' and his speeches, as a back-bencher, on the unwisdom of imposing mergers from Whitehall.

In essence the position was that the Aden ministers who favoured the merger lacked popular support, and the most articulate spokesmen of public opinion wanted not South Arabia but union with revolutionary Yemen (in the Protectorate states there was much sympathy with the Royalist Yemen, which gives an indication of the wide gulf between Colony and Protectorate). The British Government could not accept the idea of merger with the Yemen, for obvious strategic reasons, and therefore decided to force the federal merger through, out of pure British self-interest, while trying to convince people that it was being done in the interests of the Adeni people who must be helped in spite of themselves. Unfortunately the matter was complicated by the fact that Mr. Duncan Sandys—a man not easily swayed from his views—had himself decided that the merger was a good idea, and was not to be moved from this belief. Furthermore, much of the advice which he received from the men on the spot supported his attitude—and followed the British official habit of seeing the established feudal rulers as 'good Arabs' and the noisy politicians as a distasteful rabble.

In his book *The View from Steamer Point** Sir Charles Johnston confirms this point. He describes the defection of one member of the Government side in the Legislative Council before the vote on the August 1962 merger agreement, under the influence of intimidation by opponents of the merger, and adds: 'One more would have left the local members [i.e. both nominated and elected] evenly divided in the voting on the opposition amendment, and would have made it politically difficult for the Government to proceed. It was certainly a narrow escape.' Sir Charles then refers to the revolution in the Yemen after the death of the Imam Ahmed on September 19 and the joyful reaction among Aden Yemenis to the overthrowing by a coup of his successor Prince Badr. He comments:

If the Yemeni revolution had come one day earlier, or the Legislative Council vote one day later, I feel pretty certain that the London Agreement would never have obtained the support of a majority of local members. In the new atmosphere at least one more Government supporter would have defected to the opposition. Although grim to look back on, the closeness of this shave at least justified retrospectively our instinctive sense of urgency over the whole merger exercise . . . One less midnight session in Church House, and the plan might not have gone through at all. It is a solemn thought!

I was discussing this soon after the book appeared in the summer of 1964 with a senior Colonial Office official, and his comment was: 'Yes, it just shews what it all really amounted to.' Sir Charles's attitude, it seems to me, is a graphic illustration of the unreality of British policy. It is really quite extraordinary that in the 1960s any British Government should have thought it sensible to force a major constitutional reorganization through with only the lukewarm support of an unrepresentative legislature, in the face of admittedly strong popular opposition. It is even more extraordinary that anyone in a responsible place in Whitehall should have assumed for a moment that such a reorganization would have any permanent validity.

The merger of Aden with the Federation took place on January 18, 1963. Discussions then took place in Aden State on the franchise for the next elections (already postponed, as I have explained above). The elections should now have taken place in

* Collins, 1964.

January 1964. In October 1963 a commission of inquiry set up by the Chief Minister of Aden put forward recommendations, restricting the franchise to those born in Aden (ruling out, for example, Federal citizens as well as immigrant Yemeni workers) and rejecting the existing system by which people could qualify for the vote by residence and standing. While the Franchise Bill was going through the legislature, it was announced that later provisions would be made to enable Federal subjects to qualify for Aden citizenship. The process of putting the proposals into effect, however, proved too much for the Aden legislature and administration, and a further extension was made by Order in Council to the life of the legislature (a move which the British Government had, only a few months before, undertaken not to make). This time, the existing legislature was to continue until July 1964, and a new election to be held soon after that.

At Christmas 1963 there was a serious bomb incident at Aden Airport when the High Commissioner (as the Governor was now styled) was leaving for London for constitutional talks. The talks were postponed. In February 1964 the High Commissioner, Sir Kennedy Trevaskis (who had succeeded Sir Charles Johnston) visited London for 'consultations' with Mr. Sandys. By this time, misgivings about the Aden and Federal arrangements were growing rapidly. Already in the autumn of 1962 the Labour Party, then in opposition, had been highly critical of the manner in which the union had been forced through and as I have explained on the Conservative side of the House, too, there were grave doubts about the British Government's policy. The double postponement of the elections and the bomb incident in Aden were signs of the dissatisfaction and discontent which were becoming ever more pronounced in Aden itself. It extended to British Overseas Civil Servants, seconded to the Federal Civil Service, among whom there were serious criticisms both of the conditions of service and of the degree of control exercised over individual careers by the Supreme Council of the Federation (the Federal cabinet). There was also the feeling that the protection of their interests by the High Commissioner was inadequate in practice.

In the meantime, the Federal Government had been taking on more responsibilities, and the first stirrings of constitutional advance were taking place in some of the protectorate states, notably Fadhli and Lahej.

The fact remained nevertheless that the Federation was an ill assorted and heterogeneous collection of states, held together in a constitutional framework that constantly threatened to come apart at the seams. To give it more cohesion, further constitutional discussions were necessary and a new date was fixed, in June 1964, for the conference postponed by the Christmas bomb incident. In May, Mr. Sandys visited the area for one of his energetic 'see for yourself tours' (fitting it in amid other constitutional preoccupations, particularly with Basutoland, Southern Rhodesia, Northern Rhodesia and Malta) In a statement in the House of Commons on Thursday, May 14, 1962, Mr. Sandys referred to a common feeling in Aden and the Federation that South Arabia should advance towards independence 'though there were differences among them regarding the timing and the circumstances under which this should be achieved'. He announced the date for the postponed conference and then said:

It was not to be expected that the union between Aden and the Federation could be accomplished without any strains and anxieties. I was, however, encouraged to find that nobody expressed any desire to see Aden separated from the Federation. It now seems generally accepted that the peoples of Aden and of the rest of South Arabia belong together and that the well-being of all depends upon close and effective cooperation.

Unfortunately, however general might be acceptance of the ideal of close and effective cooperation, it did not in practice seem likely to work out. As a further preliminary to the June conference, Mr. Nigel Fisher went to Aden at the end of May for informal talks. His official purpose was to sound out views in Aden State, particularly among those groups who were not to be directly represented in London, about the relationship with the Federation. This meant in effect that his charm and friendliness was to be employed to try and ensure a smoother passage for the conference discussions–a role for which his extremely amiable personality was better suited than Mr. Sandys's direct and impatient approach. On the eve of Mr. Fisher's departure from London, the People's Socialist Party, led by Abdullah al Asnag, announced that they would boycott his visit. The P.S.P. had a wide following, especially within the trade unions. They were the major political party in Aden, and enjoyed the backing of Cairo. They were a self-confident political organization in a way which the collection of individuals making up the

L

Aden Government were not. They were not invited to the London conference. The reason for this was that the conference was to be a gathering of governments, not of parties, but however logical such an arrangement might seem on paper, the exclusion of the P.S.P. from deliberations affecting the whole future of South Arabia was an incredible piece of folly by a British Government which had the dismal lessons of Central Africa at that moment before it.

Just before the conference opened, Mr. al Asnag, as president of the P.S.P. and general secretary of the Aden Trade Union Congress, delivered a memorandum to Mr. Sandys, and at a press conference in London he called for representative governments to be elected in both Aden and the other states of the Federation. He described the relationship between the Aden Government and the British Government as similar to that between servant and master. While agreeing that he and his supporters favoured unity for the whole area, Mr. al Asnag added: 'We are against the present federation because it has a machinery which is left entirely in the hands of feudal lords.'

In their long memorandum to Mr. Sandys, the P.S.P. called for the implementation of the United Nations Resolution number 1949, of December 11, 1963, which described the maintenance of the military base in Aden as being prejudicial to the security of the region, and recommended (among many other clauses):

that the people of Aden and the Aden Protectorates should be allowed to exercise their right to self-determination with regard to their future, the exercise of that right to take the form of a consultation of the whole population to be held as soon as possible on the basis of universal adult suffrage.

Mr. al Asnag put across similar views on a number of occasions in the next few days, and obtained for them a good deal of publicity. He also managed to keep himself extremely well-informed about what was going on in the secrecy of the conference room, having, it appeared, a friend at court within the Aden Government delegation.

The conference got off to a bad start when Mr. Z. A. Baharoon, at that time Chief Minister of Aden, emphasized in his speech at the public opening session the differences rather than the similarities between Aden and the rest of the Federation. The people of

Aden, he said, were keen to retain the democratic organizations they had been building up over a long period. 'Moreover, it is our sincere desire and wish to see these vital instruments of political life introduced in our sister states of the Federation of South Arabia.' In a short speech, he repeated this point twice more. Mr. Baharoon also said that the existing constitution was unsatisfactory in its working.

The people of Aden were amongst the first to advocate the creation of a Federation consisting of not only Aden and the other Federal states, but also including states of the Eastern Aden Protectorate. We have gone further and have not only advocated a Federation but have looked forward with great anxiety to the creation of a unitary state, that is, a single government for South Arabia.

In essence, the line taken by Mr. Baharoon was not greatly different from that of the P.S.P.

The conference ended, after several weeks of tempestuous progress, on July 4. The report (Cmnd 2414) recorded agreement on a date for independence not later than 1968. The Federal constitution was to be reshaped on democratic lines, with a system of direct election to the National Assembly 'wherever this is practicable', though this was a matter for the individual states to decide, the alternative being a system of indirect election. There would be a president, who would be a constitutional head of state (that is, he would have to act in most things on the Prime Minister's advice). The constitutional status of Aden would be raised to that of the other states of the Federation and a meeting would be convened 'as soon as practicable after the forthcoming elections in Aden' to 'agree arrangements for the transfer of sovereignty and to settle other constitutional questions, including the basis of representation in the National Assembly . . .' This meeting would discuss also a defence agreement to enable Britain to fulfil her international obligations. In other words, Britain would retain sovereignty over the Aden base. The constitutional agreement was somewhat overshadowed by the defection, at the same weekend, of the Sultan of Fadhli, who went to Cairo, announcing his intention of seceding from the Federation. Ironically, under the rotation system in force under the old constitution, under which there was no prime minister, he was the current chairman of the Supreme Council of the Federation and as such leader of the Federal delegation to the conference.

Not only was the agreement overshadowed; it was quite unrealistic, since it quickly proved impossible to work. The attacks by Cairo on South Arabia and British policy there were increased. They were physical as well as propaganda attacks.

When the Labour Party came to office in October 1964, Mr. Anthony Greenwood, who had the portfolio of the Colonies, once again separated from Commonwealth Relations, visited Aden to have talks with all the political parties, including the P.S.P., having recognized, as the Conservative Government had failed to do, that no solution to the problems of South Arabia would work unless all the major parties were concerned in it. As a result of his talks, he announced a change of policy–in line with the Aden state Government's proposals at the July conference, South Arabia was to develop not as a federation but as a unitary state.

Soon afterwards, Sir Kennedy Trevaskis was replaced as High Commissioner by Sir Richard Turnbull, who had been Governor of Tanganyika at the time of independence (and stayed on as a much respected Governor-General) and who previously had been a brilliant and dedicated provincial commissioner in the Northern Frontier District of Kenya.

Since then, developments in the area have gone from bad to worse. In 1965 abortive attempts were made to obtain agreement on the basis for a further constitutional conference. The Aden State Government, now led by Mr. Abdul Qawee Mackawee, refused to cooperate, standing firmly and without qualifications on the U.N. resolution of December 11, 1963. Terrorism increased. Assassinations occurred, including that of Sir Arthur Charles, Speaker of the Aden Legislature, in September 1965. Eventually, at the end of September, as the security situation grew worse and the Aden elected ministers failed to condemn terrorism carried out by the National Liberation Front, Sir Richard Turnbull was authorized by the British Government to rule direct. The constitution was suspended.

No responsible government could tolerate the situation that had arisen in Aden, and however distasteful and illiberal the action might seem, the Labour Government clearly had no alternative to suspending the Aden constitution. But why had things developed to the point where this was necessary?

The basic reason is simple. In formulating a policy for Aden and the Federation, the British Government, at least until Labour came to power in 1964, were obsessed with Britain's strategic and economic interests and in consequence failed to see, or chose to ignore, the political realities of South Arabia. The manner in which the Federal union was consummated, the refusal to submit the plan to the Aden electorate until they could be presented with a *fait accompli*, the exclusion of the P.S.P. from the 1964 constitutional talks, all these were signs that Britain was determined to shape the Federation in a particular way, regardless of popular feelings if these happened to want something different.

There is nothing wrong in acting from national self-interest. All nations do it when they can, and any government has the duty to do its best for the people it governs. The great mistake in Aden was not the decision to protect British interests, so much as the errors of judgment that were made in assessing what those interests were and how best to protect them. Whatever a treaty may say, no base is of any value if it cannot be used, and its use in an emergency depends on the willing acquiescence of the local government and population. This can be assured only if the local government really represents local popular feeling. In Aden, local feeling was fanned and encouraged by Cairo and by the ideals of Arab nationalism, and to ignore that fact was to invite trouble. Of course, inviting the P.S.P. to the 1964 conference and holding an election in Aden, on a wide franchise, before the merger with the Federation, might not have produced results satisfactory to Britain. The vote might well have gone against merger. The P.S.P. which merged in 1965 with the Taiz-based Organization for the Liberation of the Occupied South, might well have remained intransigent (though usually the more extreme views expressed publicly by nationalist politicians prove to be bargaining positions from which a compromise can be arrived at, if the bargaining begins early enough, and provided that the holders of the extreme views are not antagonized before the bargaining begins). It would be foolish to suggest that if the policy had been different, there would have been no difficulties in Aden. But by refusing to accept political realities, by backing 'moderates' who could not possibly carry the people, the Conservative Government made failure inevitable.

The Labour Government tried to regain the initiative by the changes mentioned above, but it was too late. The nationalists were able to take the initiative. Symbolically, when Mr. Baharoon resigned as Chief Minister in February 1965, after a disagreement with Sir Richard Turnbull, his successor–chosen because he enjoyed the support of a majority of the legislature–was Mr. Mackawee, who had long been opposed to the idea of a merger of Aden with the other Federal states, who was strongly critical of British policy and who had been in London at the time of the conference in the summer of 1964 denouncing it as a sham. Mr. Mackawee's Government initiated a policy of militant criticism of the British Government, which rapidly developed into the chaos of terrorism which led to the suspension of the constitution in September 1965.

With independence promised for South Arabia for 1968, the Federation in effect simply disintegrated. The marriage of Aden and the protectorate states never got beyond a stormy honeymoon. Many of the circumstances which brought this about were, it is true, beyond any British Government's control, but though White- hall could not shape events, it should have been able to sense their direction. Furthermore, there should have been a far more realistic analysis of British interests. Quite apart from its usefulness in face of a hostile population, was the Aden base strategically necessary? On August 7, 1965, Mr. Anthony Greenwood, the Colonial Secre- tary reiterated (on the breakdown of talks intended to produce an agenda for a constitutional conference) that such defence interests as the British Government might have in the area after inde- pendence could be maintained only 'with the consent of the people of the area expressed through their legitimate government'. This is hardly the approach one would expect if the base was considered to be vital at all costs. Indeed, it bears out the opinion of many military experts that the base was not in any way essential, an opinion which was given official recognition in the 1966 Defence White Paper. In these circumstances, British policy on Aden and South Arabia in recent years appears not just to have failed but to have been futile.

In Central Africa and in South Arabia Britain pursued unviable policies. In Malaysia the failures were not due so directly to posi- tive action on the British Government's part, but more to a failure to take the warning signs seriously enough.

Talks on the Malaysia proposal (which had come from Tunku Abdul Rahman, the Prime Minister of Malaya), began in London under Mr. Macmillan's chairmanship in November 1961 (the time when the demise of the Rhodesia and Nyasaland Federation had been hastened by the decision to reopen negotiations on the Northern Rhodesia constitution). The British Government welcomed the Tunku's initiative. In detail Britain had two main concerns – her defence commitments both bilateral and under the South East Asia Treaty Organization, for which the Singapore bases were important, and her direct responsibility for the constitutional development of North Borneo (now Sabah) and Sarawak. Legally, Britain was also still responsible for Singapore, but there the constitution was advanced, and the existence of an elected government meant that the decision could be left in the hands of the people. (In September 1962 a referendum in Singapore produced a large majority in favour of joining Malaysia, which Mr. Lee Kuan Yew, the Singapore Prime Minister, strongly urged.) At the end of the 1961 talks agreement was reached for Britain to retain the bases 'for the purpose of assisting in the defence of Malaysia, and for Commonwealth defence and for the preservation of peace in South-East Asia', a formula which preserved the British Government's freedom to meet SEATO commitments, while enabling the Tunku to avoid any mention of SEATO, which would have at once made his position difficult among the non-aligned countries of the Afro-Asian group. From the beginning, incidentally, the concept of Malaysia had been criticized in many quarters as a neo-colonialist creation, and the right-wing predilections of the Tunku encouraged the growth of this kind of criticism. (Non-aligned countries are always more acceptable if they lean to the left than if they incline to the right, for the perfectly sound reason that the rejection of colonial rule – a recent and definite fact – is a more obviously necessary part of a non-aligned politician's equipment than is wariness against the imperialist ambitions of the communist powers – which constitute only an indefinite supposition of future intentions.)

In July and August 1962 (at the same time as the Aden merger talks), Mr. Sandys presided over discussions on the Malaysia proposal. These resulted in agreement between the British and Malayan Governments that the federation should come into being on August 31, 1963. The two governments decided that within six months (i.e. by February 1963) a formal agreement would provide for the transfer of sovereignty in North Borneo, Sarawak

and Singapore by August 31, 1963; for a definition of the relationship between Singapore and the new federation; for formal defence
agreements on the basis of the 1961 discussions and for detailed
constitutional arrangements, including safeguards for the special
interests of North Borneo and Sarawak, to be drawn up after
consultation with the legislatures in these territories. There was
agreement also on a transition period after the transfer of sovereignty, during which a number of Federal responsibilities would
be temporarily vested in the state governments. At this stage, in
August 1962, neither North Borneo nor Sarawak enjoyed full
internal self-government, the normal prelude to independence,
and Mr. Sandys announced in the House of Commons that it
would have to be introduced in both territories before the transfer
of sovereignty. Neither territory was, indeed, at all advanced constitutionally, and one of the obvious dangers in the merger–which,
to be fair, was appreciated–was that they would achieve their
independence in a marriage with the other states of Malaysia
without having had the opportunity, normal with British colonial
territories, of expressing an opinion through a fully representative
parliament. Combined with this was the existence of racial suspicion, throughout the proposed federation, between the Malays,
the Chinese and the indigenous peoples of the Borneo territories.

The need to assess opinion in the Borneo territories had been
recognized, and a Commission under Lord Cobbold had spent
two months in the area sounding out the views of the people.
The Cobbold report (Cmnd 1794) was published on August 1,
1962, simultaneously with Mr. Sandys's announcement of the
agreements achieved at the conference. The Commission, consisting of British and Malayan government representatives, agreed
in principle that Malaysia would be a good idea, though there
were differences between the British and Malayan representatives
on details of timing. The Commission recommended specific
measures to safeguard the rights of the Borneo peoples. The
chairman's summing-up of views in the Borneo territories on
Malaysia was as follows:

About one third of the population in each territory strongly favours
early realization of Malaysia without too much concern about terms and
conditions. Another third, many of them favourable to the Malaysia
project, ask, with varying degrees of emphasis, for conditions and safeguards varying in nature and extent . . . The remaining third is divided

between those who insist on independence before Malaysia is considered and those who would strongly prefer to see British rule continue for some years to come . . . Once a firm decision was taken quite a number of the third category would be likely to abandon their opposition and decide to make the best of a doubtful job. There will remain a hard core, vocal and politically active, which will oppose Malaysia on any terms unless it is preceded by independence and self-government; this hard core might amount to nearly 20 per cent of the population and some-what less in North Borneo.

When one considers the difficulties of making any Federal system work, and adds to them the peculiar problems when the constituent parts of the federation are separated by ocean as well as by ethnic and cultural gulfs and constitutional development, one appreciates that the implications of the Cobbold report were not altogether encouraging. There were serious risks in going ahead with the Malaysia scheme and though it could reasonably be argued that the risks were in the circumstances worth taking, it was important to understand them and to take all possible steps to reduce them.

There was a further conference in June and July 1963 to agree the complicated constitutional arrangements, and difficulties arose at this point over financial and fiscal matters between Singapore (economically far in advance of the rest of the Federation, in-cluding Malaya) and Malaya. They ended in compromise, thanks largely to the mediation of Mr. Duncan Sandys in the chair. Finally, when all was signed and sealed, President Sukarno of Indonesia began his virulent campaign against Malaysia by de-manding a United Nations investigation of the views of the people of North Borneo and Sarawak. Reluctantly the Tunku and the British Government agreed to an investigation (with the face-saving formula that it was carried out by representatives of U Thant, the U.N. Secretary-General, personally rather than by representatives of the U.N. itself). To enable it to take place, the birth of Malaysia was delayed from August 31 to September 16, 1963.

The peculiar difficulties of Malaysia can be summed-up quite simply. There was—and is—antagonism between the Chinese and the Malays, arising out of the predominance of the Malays politi-cally and of the Chinese economically, and the long-standing determination of the Malays not to be ousted by the Chinese.

Related to this racial antagonism is the specific resentment of the Borneo territories to political domination by Kuala Lumpur and the Malays. Already in 1961 Colonial Office officials were reporting the strong desire among a substantial section of the population of Sarawak and North Borneo (particularly Sarawak) for much greater powers to remain in state rather than central hands, including control of immigration and education. This problem was exacerbated by the shortage of trained administrators from the Borneo territories, which meant that either the British colonial administrators must remain, or they must be replaced by Malays. Of the two choices, the local preference was for the British, on the 'devil we know' principle. Then, the original concept of Malaysia had to be revised when it became clear that the Sultan of Brunei, who is under British protection, but not British sovereignty, had no intention of taking his state into the Federation. Finally, as I have mentioned, the idea of Malaysia was opposed from without, and the reality of Malaysia was attacked and subverted by Indonesia. These attacks, and the propaganda that went with them, were helped by the fact that Britain's defence strategy, and her international responsibilities in South-East Asia, have been held to depend on the existence of bases in Singapore. The continuing military presence of the former colonial power is a gift to the critics of neo-colonialism.

With these problems and difficulties so fundamental to the Malaysia concept, it behoved any British Government to be careful. The major mistake that was made by Whitehall was to over-emphasize the preservation of the integrity of Malaysia as the reason for the presence of large British forces in the area. Certainly the defence of Malaysia against Indonesian attacks has been one of the main functions of these British forces, but it is not the only function; unfortunately the spontaneous fission that dismembered Malaysia in August 1965 gave legitimate grounds for questioning whether the integrity of Malaysia had ever been more than an invention of the constitutional draughtsmen. If Malaysia had been considered in isolation, Whitehall's error of judgment would have been entirely understandable. Against the background of crumbling or abortive federations that was such a feature of 1961 and 1962, the error ought not to have been made.

Chapter 12

The Smaller Territories

ON February 18, 1965, The Gambia became an independent member of the Commonwealth. Exactly one week later, on February 25, Mr. Anthony Greenwood, the Colonial Secretary, spoke about Britain's remaining dependencies at a meeting of Commonwealth Writers of Britain. The territories, he suggested, fell into three groups.

There are the ones which affect our foreign relations—Gibraltar, South Arabia and the Falkland Islands are examples. There are those where the situation is made more difficult by racial mistrust—and where we are expected to hold the ring. Finally there are those whose geographical position and whose lack of natural resources make it difficult for them to be viable units without considerable injections of aid and investment from outside.

It would have been tactless, but true, if Mr. Greenwood had chosen that moment to point out that The Gambia, newly independent, came well below what one might call the threshold of viability. The Gambia is a geographical absurdity. It is 300 miles long, and yet at its widest point only 30 miles wide. It consists of a thin strip of land on either bank of the Gambia river. Apart from its narrow length of sea coast, the country is entirely surrounded by Senegal. Ethnic and religious links between Senegal and The Gambia are close. The administrative and cultural traditions of the two countries, however, reflect closely those of the former tutelary powers. Dakar is as French a city as one could find outside France. Bathurst, though a village rather than a city, is English down to the cricket ground immediately outside the government headquarters. Economically both countries are weak, depending heavily on the export of peanuts for which the market is unfavourable. The Gambia's weakness is such that the country is kept economically alive only by continual infusions of British Government money. (Senegal depends similarly, though not quite

167

so totally, on French aid.) Anyone looking objectively at the possibilities of changing The Gambia's economic condition finds little to encourage him. Even an excellent booklet prepared in May 1963 by the Gambia Government, though it makes the best of things, is quite candid about the situation.

Gambia has good potential, which is as yet unexploited, as a winter tourist resort. Bathurst town is very short of up-to-date houses, flats and offices, and site values are fairly low for a capital city, even of a small country. The beautiful Atlantic coast is wholly unspoilt and only a small part of the adjacent land is occupied by the villas erected by the Government and overseas firms for their staff . . . Building, contracting, hotels, catering and service facilities generally await development . . . In agriculture there seems to be scope for developing citrus, mangoes, avocado pears and other tropical orchard fruit for export . . . Opportunities for establishing light industries in Gambia are restricted by the smallness of the home market, but the rapid political evolution of West Africa, including the prospects of closer association with Senegal, may well increase the advantages offered by this country . . . Gambia has few proved mineral resources . . .

This is a brave document, but it is—regrettably though inevitably—a catalogue of unfulfilled hopes.

The proposal for a form of association with Senegal has been canvassed for a number of years and after Senegal's independence in 1960 committees of ministers from both countries began to meet regularly to discuss functional cooperation in various fields. Eventually the British Government (acting for The Gambia, which was then still a colony) and the Senegalese Government asked the United Nations to conduct a survey of the possibilities and the difficulties of association. The report of the U.N. team reached the two governments in March 1964, and when I visited both countries in April of that year, it was both a closely guarded secret and a constant topic of conversation (a happy combination for a journalist). The U.N. recommendations were completely realistic. The team analysed the affinities between the two countries and the anomalies that their separation produced. They pointed out that maintenance of a complete separation would make a heavy demand on the material and human resources of The Gambia without opening the way to a more radical improvement of its economy that could come from basing it on a broader foundation. At the same time, Senegal would be hampered in the full development of its southern territories (the Casamance, which lies to the south of The Gambia). On the other hand, the different cultural elements, administrative practices, economic policies and fiscal and financial structures warranted a prudent approach to the problem of association. The report declared that complete political integration as the immediate goal of negotiations seemed unrealistic and would most probably not obtain the free assent of both peoples at that time. Suggesting that a federation with limited central powers might be the most logical goal as a first stage, the U.N. team added that it might be still more practical initially not to go beyond a treaty relationship creating a common international representation, a common defence and common organs for the harmonization of trade and customs policies and development plans.

From conversations during my visit it quickly became obvious that the U.N. report had simply reflected the facts and that the closer the need for decision on Senegambia came, the less enthusiasm there was for it. I wrote at the time that the British Government,

recognizing that the possibility of getting Gambian agreement to the Senegambia association hangs by a fine thread, are anxious not to encourage controversy. At the same time the Government are putting a good deal of pressure on the Gambia . . . to accept what most observers see as the only sane solution.

A few days later in the House of Commons Mr. Nigel Fisher, the Under-Secretary of State, declared that 'the Government have not and will not put any pressure upon The Gambia at all to enter any form of partnership with Senegal. Our position is that we believe that a closer association between them is a very sensible policy and we will therefore support any move towards it.' For a grant-aided territory as heavily dependent on the British taxpayer as is The Gambia, the expression of the British Government's beliefs and opinions must carry great weight, and in insisting that no pressure was brought to bear, the Government were arguing semantically. Certainly I did not feel I should have written differently.

In practice, association with Senegal has remained strictly limited, and The Gambia has entered independence as a separate entity. Britain continues to support and to subsidize, and this, in my view, is absolutely right. The Gambia was Britain's oldest West African possession and its associations with this country date back to the sixteenth century. Its anomalous shape and its undeveloped economy are certainly not the fault of the Gambians who, having been taught to respect British standards, have the right to expect that Britain will provide the means for them to do so.

The fact remains that The Gambia was launched as an unviable independent state because no one had thought out any alternative goal to aim for—except the goal of submersion in Senegambia. The concept of Senegambia, I suggest, has aroused a quite unmerited enthusiasm in Whitehall, and has in fact been used as a substitute for sensible and constructive thought. It has always been held self-evident that a marriage between Senegal and The Gambia would be to the benefit of both. Administratively, Senegal would certainly draw advantages from having the Casamance within easier reach than now, when foreign territory lies between it and Dakar. The economic advantages are far less apparent. How, for example, could the union of two weak economies, each depending on groundnuts, produce a strong economy? External subsidies would still be just as necessary as they are now, and France and Britain would be the most likely sources of aid. Again, though it is obvious from a glance at a map that the Gambia river is the natural highway for a large, French-speaking hinterland, history has been stronger than geography, and its victory is unlikely to be reversed. After all, to develop the Gambia river could not fail to be detrimental to the Senegalese ports. The fact that the two countries were one would not alter this, nor make the development any more acceptable or sensible—in today's conditions.

In any case the political arguments *against* union—from delight in the trappings of independence to the great difference in attitude inherited from the French and the British colonial rulers—are far stronger, as political arguments usually prove to be, than any economic reasons *for* it. The failure to associate should not have surprised any reasonably well-informed observer who took into account the lessons of other areas where economics has proved no match for politics. It ought not to have surprised the British Government. Neither the Colonial Office nor the Foreign Office should have had more than transient hopes that Senegambia, whose prototype failed after less than twenty years in the eighteenth century, would succeed in the twentieth.

I have suggested that Whitehall enthusiasm for the idea was a substitute for constructive thought. It was also symptomatic of the absence of constructive thinking on the whole question of the smaller and unviable territories. Yet this question did not spring upon British ministers and officials suddenly and without warning. As long ago as 1954–before Ghana's independence and not many years after India's–Sir Hilary Blood, an experienced colonial governor and constitutional expert, and one of the few senior men really to apply his mind to the problem, was concerned with conditions which would preclude a grant of independence. To an audience in Oxford in May 1965, Sir Hilary Blood recalled what these conditions were.

The first was size. It was never precisely defined, but at that time, Sierra Leone was considered to be a border-line case (with 2,450,000 inhabitants and about 28,000 square miles). Cyprus was the turning point. When it became independent in 1960, with 578,000 inhabitants in 3,572 square miles, the criterion of size ceased to matter. As Sir Hilary Blood has pointed out, the independence of Cyprus was a Foreign Office decision rather than a Colonial Office one, since it came as the solution to an international quarrel.

The second condition was strategic importance. This meant that the 'fortress colonies', places of strategic importance, could not become independent. At the time these 'fortress colonies' included Singapore, considered essential for the guarding of world trade routes. Even then, however, it was recognized that the development of modern communications and weapons would change the importance of the fortress colonies, and would indeed alter the list of such territories from time to time. Now this condition is almost totally irrelevant. The sovereign base areas in Cyprus could have little use in any but a few strictly limited types of situation. Aden's strategic value, as we have seen, is now held to be pretty low. Gibraltar, more literally than anywhere else a 'fortress colony', cannot be said to play a vital role in Britain's defence dispositions.

The third condition was a homogeneous society. A mixed society, where racial antagonisms existed, even potentially, should have its progress to independence slowed down. The two most obvious examples of mixed society colonies were British Guiana and Mauritius. In the autumn of 1965, constitutional conferences were held in London for both territories, and both were promised their independence in 1966. Yet in neither case had any real solution been found of the racial problem. In Mauritius, where a state of emergency, proclaimed in May, ended only at the beginning of August, a month before the constitutional conference, there was a fundamental cleavage between the advocates of independence and those who wanted a continuing link with Britain. The British Government, in the person of Mr. Anthony Greenwood, Colonial Secretary, rejected the idea of a referendum on the grounds that its main effect would be 'to prolong the current uncertainty and political controversy in a way which could only harden and deepen communal divisions and rivalries'.

In British Guiana there was certainly no consensus before the decision on independence. Indeed Dr. Cheddi Jagan, the former Prime Minister, refused to attend the constitutional conference. (He was defeated in elections in December 1964 held under a system of proportional representation imposed by Mr. Sandys.) Special provisions were written into the new constitution to deal with racial discrimination. In the period before independence, which it achieved in May 1966, Guyana–to use its new name–did seem to be in a rather happier state than for many years. Nevertheless, it could not be claimed that the racial problem had been settled. What all this indicates is that the third criterion for independence is now completely ignored.

The fourth condition was that there should be a large enough number of educated administrators. (There is usually no shortage of politicians. It is always easier to talk about policies than to implement them.) As a glance at any of a long list of recently independent countries will shew, independence has been granted even when nearly all senior administrative posts have had to remain in expatriate hands.

Finally, there was the economic condition. In the early 1950s, it was felt that no country could become independent if it could not at least meet its own recurrent budgetary expenditure. (Aid for capital development is a different matter.) In assessing the economic position, it must be remembered that independence itself, however modestly it is asserted, brings its own additional expenses–the cost of representation abroad, and of defence arrangements, for example. The Gambia is the most striking example of an independent country that cannot meet this fifth condition, but there are others, such as Malawi and Malta, and others still in the queue, such as Basutoland, Bechuanaland and Swaziland.

Between 1954 and the present day, therefore, all the criteria which were considered essential prerequisites of independence have been rejected. Nothing has been put in their place. Officials have been aware of the problem, and have studied its implications. Successive ministers have inevitably been too much involved with the larger colonies to pay any attention to it, though as the years passed, the moment for decisions on the future of the smaller territories loomed nearer and nearer.

At the meeting which I mentioned at the beginning of this chapter, Mr. Greenwood made what was probably the clearest declaration ever uttered by a modern Colonial Secretary discussing policy towards dependent territories. He referred to the United Nations General Assembly Resolution 1514 which states that 'inadequacy of political, economic, social or educational prepared-ness should never serve as a pretext for delaying independence' but commented that

in any particular case, such inadequacies – and they exist – may well be deterrents, both for us and for the people of the territory in question. But I entirely agree that these very real factors should not be used as a pretext or an excuse for delaying independence. For us, however, the question does not arise. For our territories, independence is not some-thing which can be conferred like an honorary degree. Indeed, the state-ment has little relevance to the way in which British territories actually advance. *Those who really want independence, get it.* The real point is that the pace of political progress is, in the last analysis, a matter for the people themselves.

He pointed out, however, that there would be a number of smaller and more remote territories which, by their own circumstances and their own free choice, would remain with Britain and a British responsibility, and 'we ought to be thinking very seriously how we should discharge our continuing responsibility in the years to come'.

Later in 1965 Mr. Greenwood obeyed his own injunction and set in train measures designed to encourage that thought. In the first place he invited four teams of M.P.s (each consisting of a Conservative and a Labour supporter) to visit a number of the

M

smaller territories as his personal representatives, and to report back to him. As the Colonial Office pointed out, although there had previously been Parliamentary missions of various kinds, this was the first occasion on which teams of M.P.s had been asked to go on a series of visits as the personal representatives of a Colonial Secretary. Mr. Greenwood himself and his Parliamentary Secretary, Mrs. Eirene White, visited some of the territories.

His second initiative was to call a conference in July 1965, at which Colonial Office officials, governors, academics, businessmen and journalists met in private in Lady Margaret Hall, Oxford, for informal discussions 'on various aspects of the future relationship between Britain and the colonial territories'. In so far as it concentrated the thoughts of a number of well-qualified men and women on the problem, this conference was a success. To what extent it was able to provide the inspiration for a realistic policy, however, is more doubtful, not because of any incapacity on the part of the participants, but because probably by the middle of 1965 it was too late to redirect the momentum of colonial change.

It is easy to make jokes about the likelihood of independence for the Pitcairn Islands Group (population 107), or even for St. Helena and its dependencies (population 4,522). But the joke seems rather less funny when one remembers that British Honduras (population 96,000) is expected to become independent. Most people would probably agree that there are some territories for which full independence makes no sense at all. The question is, where is the line to be drawn, and how can it be done in a way that is acceptable not only to Britain and the dependency concerned, but also to the United Nations? It is not an easy question to answer.

Because one set of criteria for independence was rejected and no others put in their place, any new definition of the prerequisites of independence is likely to be subject to glaring exceptions. This, after all, is how the earlier criteria came to be meaningless. Small territories have been treated on the same basis as large ones by a process of inertia. The system was there, it was known to work reasonably well, and no thought was given to the conditions that must be present before it worked well. Already this process has gone so far that it cannot be stopped in many cases where common sense would suggest that some other solution than independence would be more reasonable. It cannot be stopped because, as I have stressed earlier, the impetus to independence among non-independent peoples is not governed by economic factors nor by logic, but by political factors and emotions. I am not at all sure that it could have been stopped even if the situation had been reappraised in the 1950s, before independence had become a colonial commonplace. I am sure that the facts should have been examined and assessed so that in setting whatever goal was agreed for the smaller territories the British Government could have tried to ensure that suitable preparations were made.

The full results of the failure to make this examination and to set these preparations in train have yet to be seen. One example of decades of failure to grasp reality is Southern Rhodesia. This, of course, is not a 'small territory' in the sense in which we are using the term, but behind the crisis which broke in November 1965 with the seizure of illegal independence by Ian Smith and his collaborators lay years of unwillingness by successive British Governments to give any reality to the principles which they all proclaimed. All expressed their belief in democratic methods, in protection of human rights and above all in the fact that Britain was ultimately responsible for Southern Rhodesia. At the same time, while successive Southern Rhodesian Governments betrayed these principles, eroded democracy, ignored human rights and cocked snooks at Whitehall, no British Government was prepared to put its foot down. Indeed, they were all bemused by the 'parliamentary convention' that Whitehall did not interfere in Rhodesia and sometimes seemed to revel in the ludicrous fact that Britain had responsibility but had steadily given away the power to exercise it.

In quite different circumstances one can foresee similar rude awakenings on the horizon. I have already mentioned the case of Malawi, which entered independence with little money, little to develop and precious few preparations for Malawians to take over the administration. Britain, as I have explained, pays–and will probably have to go on paying indefinitely. The same is true, only more so, of The Gambia. But has any British Government thought out the full implications of this? Is the British taxpayer willing to pay indefinitely? There is an undoubted moral responsibility to continue to provide help to countries which it suited Britain at one time to possess–but has this moral responsibility been thoroughly understood even by our legislators? Even more pertinently, has it been put across properly to the public? The answer, regrettably, is no.

An even more obvious source of trouble to come is the situation of the three High Commission territories of Swaziland, Basutoland and Bechuanaland. The policy of granting them all independence in effect when they wished to take it was stated in the final communiqué of the Commonwealth Prime Ministers' meeting of July 1964. The relevant passage read: 'Basutoland had been promised that she could have independence in about eighteen months' time; Bechuanaland would be free to follow when she wished; and Swaziland's new constitution had now set her on the same course.' The precise timing of successive constitutional changes still had to be discussed. The basic decision was made. Now, the final stage has been reached, and Bechuanaland, for instance, is to become independent this year as the Republic of Botswana. Yet none of the three territories can be said to be ready for independence. They all have weak economies (with the possible exception of Swaziland). They all depend economically on South Africa, through the customs union, operated by South Africa, which provides much of their income, and by virtue of the fact that many of their citizens can find work and earn incomes only by going to the Republic. Geographically, too, they are at the mercy of South Africa. This is true most strikingly of Basutoland, which is entirely surrounded by South Africa, an island of African government in a hostile sea of white supremacy. It is scarcely less true of the other two. Swaziland's only other neighbour is Portuguese-ruled Mozambique, on which it relies for access to the sea, but in any political conflict, Portugal's sympathies are more likely to lie with South Africa than with an independent Swaziland. Bechuanaland, by far the largest of the three, has frontiers with South Africa, South West Africa (which South Africa rules) and Southern Rhodesia, all potentially hostile. It has a fifty-yard border, on the Zambesi, with Zambia, but although this window on a friendly world has obvious advantages, it also presents problems, since it makes Bechuanaland a corridor for refugees from South Africa, and for nationalists returning to try and overthrow Dr. Verwoerd's Government by sabotage. Inevitably, therefore, Bechuanaland will always be under the threat of reprisals by South Africa.

To sum up, the three southern African territories, with the possible exception of Swaziland, are unviable geographically and economically. Politically they could not pursue any policy directly hostile to South Africa (and as independent countries they will be under much pressure to adopt such policies), and what is more at any time South Africa's Government could put virtually irresistible pressures on them to pursue policies favourable to South Africa. At any time, their access to the outside world could be cut off by South Africa. This in fact has happened, with the refusal by South Africa to allow certain citizens of the territories to cross South African territory, as they must do in order to return home from abroad. This has occurred at a time when the territories were under full British control and short of going to war with South Africa, the British Government was powerless to persuade South Africa to permit the travellers through. With the territories independent, Britain's power must be even less.

Great play has been made with the fact that the political leaders in the High Commission territories have taken a 'statesmanlike' line over relations with South Africa, but it is hard to see what other line they could have taken. It is painfully clear that Britain, in granting them independence, is quite unable to guarantee that independence in any meaningful way. Apart from the logistic difficulties in the way of providing any form of military assistance against a threat by South Africa, no British Government would like to risk the domestic political consequences of committing troops to such a purpose.

Economically, Britain can provide help, though the size of the task is enormous after years and years of neglect. The traditional British attitude to the territories is well summed up in Dudley Barker's book *Swaziland*, published in 1965 by Her Majesty's Stationery Office in the Corona Library series sponsored by the Colonial Office. Discussing the problem of leading the Swazi from their tribal isolation to a condition in which they are fit to share the control of a modern state he commented: 'The difficulty of the problem is partly due to the long period of apathy after Britain had reluctantly taken Swaziland into its protection.' He then mentions that until the Second World War both British and South African Governments assumed that the territories would be incorporated into the Union of South Africa, in spite of the opposition of the Africans in them, and he adds:

But when he [Field-Marshal Smuts] was defeated at the polls by Dr. Malan, and the Nationalist Government was formed with its policy of increasing racial segregation, public opinion in Britain was not in favour of transferring to South African rule the Africans for whom Britain had responsibility.

In 1954 the British Government (under Sir Winston Churchill) said that the transfer was out of the question, and that remained the policy of all subsequent British Governments. The apathy to which Mr. Barker refers, however, did not evaporate when the policy was changed and Britain accepted a continuing responsibility for the territories. One sign of the ambivalent attitude towards the territories that prevailed in Whitehall was the fact that they were a Commonwealth Relations Office rather than a Colonial Office responsibility, and their governor–entitled High Commissioner–was also High Commissioner to South Africa. Understandably the distinction between gubernatorial and diplomatic functions became blurred, not so much in the mind of the High Commissioner as in the corporate thinking of the C.R.O., a department not geared to the government of colonies. Another sign was that not only were the territories governed from Pretoria, but the capital of Bechuanaland itself was Mafeking, situated outside the protectorate and in the Union of South Africa.

When South Africa left the Commonwealth in 1961, the High Commissioner became an ambassador, though for a time retaining his responsibility, wearing another hat, for the three protectorates. At the end of 1961, at long last, it was decided to place them under the control of the Colonial Office, and to build a new capital for Bechuanaland at Gaberones.

These were the eleventh-hour attempts to launch the territories into a credible independence but like most eleventh-hour attempts they had only a strictly limited promise of success. To quote an article by the Commonwealth Staff of *The Times* on August 24, 1965, 'whether they will end as Verwoerdian Bantustans has to be seen'.

In drawing attention to these weaknesses, I am not suggesting that recent British Governments were in a position to alter the fundamental facts. Obviously, colonial policies after the 1939–45 war were based on totally different assumptions from those before the war. I do suggest that the inexorable logic of the situation should have been recognized far earlier than it was. Examining the implications of the geographic and economic position of Basutoland, Bechuanaland and Swaziland should have been a priority. If it had been, the absurdity of treating them just like any other colony and granting them the traditional independence would quickly have become apparent, and some new and appropriate policy could have been evolved before the momentum of history made the absurd inevitable.

With no large colonies left to worry about, Mr. Greenwood addressed himself to the problems of the smaller ones as soon as he went to the Colonial Office. The answer for them seems to lie in some form of close association with Britain–perhaps a Northern Ireland relationship, perhaps something looser, but in any event, an association which must give the colonial citizens full United Kingdom rights. With immigration laws, and the public's attitude to immigrants, in their present state, it is hard to see a solution of this kind gaining ready acceptance in Britain. But what is the alternative? Are we prepared to subsidize the smallest island in all the trappings of sovereign independence, including a vote at the United Nations? Or are we simply to slide out of our responsibilities and leave our colonial charges, in an anti-colonial era, in a kind of under-developed slum of anomaly? That is what is implicit in the new West Indies form of association, mentioned above, unless it is combined with full citizenship rights.

Chapter *13*

The Commonwealth - Fact or Fiction?

THE avowed aim of British colonial policy in recent years has been the granting of independence, and as I emphasized early in this book, independence carries with it the right to pursue any policy one chooses. In practice, nearly every former British territory on becoming independent has chosen to remain within the Commonwealth. Apart from Burma, the exceptions have had special practical reasons for not staying (British Somaliland because of its marriage with Italian Somaliland to form the Somali Republic; the Southern Cameroons, because they chose union with the former French Cameroon Republic to form the Federal Republic of Cameroon). Even when independence was followed by an upheaval and a change of constitutional status, as in the case of Malaysia, or of Zanzibar, the new constitutional entities sought Commonwealth membership. This is one indication of the great flexibility of the Commonwealth, which was first clearly established in 1949 when the Commonwealth Prime Ministers' meeting accepted India as a continuing Commonwealth member, in spite of her decision to change from monarchy with the Queen as Head of State to republic. Since then, many other Commonwealth countries have become republics, usually after a period of independence as monarchies but in one case (Zambia) immediately. Cyprus became independent as a republic, but did not join the Commonwealth until nearly a year later.

If flexibility is one of the most obvious features of the Commonwealth another is that over the years, and particularly since the Second World War, it has completely changed its character. This is of course a frequently repeated truism. The transformation of an all-white club of nations all holding broadly the same political views and pursuing the same policies into a multi-racial gathering of *prima donna* states, all pursuing different ones, is portrayed as

180

a success story or a sign of decadence, depending on one's point of view. (The success story is the more usual.) Because of the great increase in the number of members, quite apart from the differences between their policies, the regular Commonwealth Prime Ministers' gatherings have become large-scale set pieces, rather than intimate 'cabinet discussions'. The whole apparatus of aides and press officers, public statements and interviews, makes intimacy impossible.

It is easy enough to say what the changed Commonwealth is not. It is not, for example, a political unit. It is not an economic grouping; not all its members even belong to the sterling area, and some non-members do. In the 1964 edition of *The Commonwealth Relations Office List* the negative attributes of the Commonwealth were clearly stated in a passage which set out to describe the Commonwealth positively. It reads:

> The Commonwealth thus possesses a unique character, distinguishing it from any other form of association of States. It differs from a federation, since there is no central executive government, legislature or judiciary. . . . There are, with few exceptions, no contractual obligations existing between members . . . even on such vital matters as mutual assistance in war or concerted action in threatening circumstances. *There is no legal or formal obstacle to any member pursuing a policy diametrically opposed to that of any other member.* [my italics]. What holds the Commonwealth together is . . . a community of ideals and interests shared by all alike and a voluntary determination to cooperate on all issues on which agreement is possible.

The article then lists some of the common interests: a broadly similar legislative pattern and parliamentary procedure; the fact that the Queen is head of the executive in all Commonwealth governments except the republics, Malaysia, Uganda and Zanzibar (this was before the merger of Zanzibar and Tanganyika); a broadly similar system of law; discrimination in favour of Commonwealth citizens in nationality laws; a process of continuous consultation between Commonwealth countries.

Some of these common interests and ideals are largely mythical. Commonwealth members *do* pursue policies that are diametrically opposed to those of other Commonwealth members. The list of issues 'on which agreement is possible' grows steadily smaller.

It is worth examining in rather more detail the common interests mentioned in the *C.R.O. List* article.

A SIMILAR LEGISLATIVE PATTERN AND
PARLIAMENTARY PROCEDURE

The article itself mentions some exceptions—Ghana, Pakistan and to some extent Cyprus. In the light of subsequent developments one must add Tanzania, which has an avowed and specially devised (and incidentally quite effective) one-party system in which voters may choose between different candidates all representing the same party. The list would also include Zambia, which entered independence with a special presidential system. There is a case for adding Kenya, which has a presidential system of government and is *de facto* a one-party state. In listing these exceptions I am not implying any criticism. There seems to be no good reason why Zambia, for example, should have the same legislative and parliamentary pattern as Britain. But whatever the judgment, the fact remains that of the twenty-two independent Commonwealth states in existence at the end of 1965, at least six do not share this particular common interest.

THE POSITION OF THE QUEEN

To claim the Queen's position as head of the executive as a sign of the common pattern of Commonwealth interests is utterly ludicrous, since there are more exceptions than adherents to the pattern. Of the twenty-two members, the following are republics: India, Pakistan, Ghana, Nigeria, Cyprus, Tanzania, Kenya, Zambia. Uganda, though it does not call itself a republic, has a President as head of state. Malaysia is an elective monarchy, with the headship of state rotating among the Malay rulers. Malawi, The Gambia and Singapore have announced their intention of becoming republics. The total of these is thirteen. Of the remaining nine which are monarchies with the Queen as head of state, Ceylon and Sierra Leone may well change to republican status.

THE SYSTEM OF LAW

The *C.R.O. List* mentions as an exception to the common legal system Ceylon, where the basis is Roman Dutch law, not English common law. One would now have to add Malta (which became independent after this particular edition of the list was published) where, again, the common law system does not operate. The exceptions under this heading are sufficiently few to make it a valid example of common interests, though the ostensible forms do not always reflect the realities. Faith in the rule of law in Ghana, for example, was seriously undermined when President Nkrumah dismissed Sir Arku Korsah as Chief Justice after a court over which he presided delivered a politically unpopular verdict. (For the details, see Chapter 1.)

NATIONALITY DIFFERENTIATION

Strictly speaking discrimination in favour of fellow Commonwealth citizens can be claimed as a feature of the Commonwealth countries. It is a feature which was always limited by the fact that many of them had, and still have, strongly restrictive immigration laws. Canada has allowed people from Britain, Australia and New Zealand to enter as immigrants with little formality. With other Commonwealth countries there are usually quota arrangements. Australia has long had its white Australia policy. Most other Commonwealth countries have some sort of restriction, usually tied to the ability of the immigrant to support himself. It is getting more difficult for expatriates to enter the far eastern Commonwealth countries. In 1962 Britain herself, having for years allowed free entry for any Commonwealth citizen, introduced the Commonwealth Immigrants Act, an illiberal measure which the Labour Party, then in opposition, attacked—but whose illiberality they decided to increase when they came to power in 1964. The policy of discrimination in favour of Commonwealth citizens, however true in practice, has certainly not seemed to be true, and can hardly therefore be claimed as a unifying common interest.

CONTINUOUS CONSULTATION

The continuous process of full and frank consultation is frequently held up as one of the most beneficent features of the Commonwealth. From time to time, ministers have mentioned the thousands of telegrams that pour in and out of the Commonwealth Relations Office in the course of a year. It is certainly true that consultation is easier between Commonwealth countries than between fully foreign countries. For one thing, High Commissioners have greater rights of approach to ministers in the countries to which they are accredited than do ambassadors. But if one considers the quality of consultation, the picture is rather different. On many of the most urgent and important issues of international diplomacy there is none at all. Can anyone pretend, for example, that in formulating defence policies Britain exchanges more secrets with The Gambia or Malawi than with the United States? It would be absurd and irresponsible if she did. Failures to consult are not of course all one way. If there was any prior consultation by Ghana when she decided to form the Ghana–Guinea–Mali union, those who were consulted in Whitehall managed to keep the secret from their colleagues, who read about the union in the newspapers. Again, there was no real reason why Ghana should have consulted other Commonwealth members first, with the possible exception of Nigeria. All nations, after all, have specific interests with particular neighbours. As I write, a further strain has been imposed on the flexibility of the Commonwealth, and a further dilution has taken place in the quality of Commonwealth consultation, by the decision of Tanzania and Ghana to obey a resolution of the Organization of African Unity and break diplomatic relations with Britain over the question of Southern Rhodesia. This is the first instance of a breach in diplomatic relations between Commonwealth members. Even when India and Pakistan have been effectively at war with each other, they have continued to maintain missions in each other's capitals. (Ghana has since resumed relations.)

One of the greatest mistakes made by many in thinking about the Commonwealth is to assume that in its modern form, and with its diverse and numerous membership, it can be a kind of extension of Britain. The assumption is made most consciously by the right-wing romantics, who like to think of a club of like-minded white men, with similar democratic institutions, and would allow into membership only those black and brown men who make the grade by accepting and adopting the white rules. An extreme form of this attitude can be seen in those who openly or tacitly supported Mr. Ian Smith when he overthrew Southern Rhodesia's constitution in November 1965. Most of these people would be horrified at the thought of condoning either illegality or injustice, yet they could not believe that a group of white men–their own kith and kin, many of whom had good war records–could deliberately break the law and introduce repressive measures of a kind which Hitler had employed. Even among people who reject everything which this right-wing irresponsible fringe hold dear, however, there is often a tendency to assume that the Commonwealth is meaningful only in so far as it reflects a British way of life. It is, indeed, a natural tendency for the British, who are justly well satisfied with the standards on which our way of life is based. Nevertheless it is not realistic.

After the 1965 Commonwealth Prime Ministers' meeting, Dr. Eric Williams of Trinidad and Tobago had some astringent things to say about Britain's 'proprietary' attitude to the Commonwealth. He referred in particular to the proposed Commonwealth mission to try and bring about peace in Vietnam of which he, like Mr. Harold Wilson, the British Prime Minister, was a member. He complained that in presenting the proposal to set up the mission, references by British ministers had been always to 'Mr. Wilson's mission'. Commonwealth problems were always analysed in terms of Britain's internal politics and Dr. Williams and other Commonwealth prime ministers felt that for the British Government the Commonwealth existed to interpret Britain's needs.

Dr. Williams is not a man who minces his words. It is not necessary to accept all his opinions, however, to see that they are based on more than a grain of truth. How often, for example, are the new Commonwealth countries awarded certificates of merit simply according to the extent to which they retain a British way of doing things, or the outward British forms, or the extent to which they adopt policies which we in Britain think reasonable? We praise the 'statesmanship' of an African leader who accepts the need for western capital or who calls on the Royal Marines to sort out a mutiny. We condemn as irresponsible a leader who wants military action against Southern Rhodesia or South Africa. Are our reactions reasonable?

The essence of sane political behaviour is realism. The leader of a country in desperate need of capital development must find capital and he is more likely to find it from the west than from the east. He probably then tries to find a compensating relationship with the east–not simply, or even primarily, because he is cynically playing one off against the other, but because the belief in non-alignment is very real to the average African politician, however eccentric and idealistic it may seem to us, conditioned as we are by the fact that we are aligned, and must be if we are to survive. But in measuring realism, no political leader can use only logical criteria or economic criteria. If politics is the art of the possible, what is possible is what people will put up with. In a dictatorship they have to put up with more than they will take in a democracy, but ultimately even the dictator is liable to be toppled from power by *coup d'état*. The question of white rule by autocratic minorities in Africa is not for Africans a matter of debate on the niceties of constitutional theory and the realities of power. It is an issue of the most fundamental principle, which an African leader ignores at his peril. To describe as irresponsible the utterances of leaders who reflect their people's deep feelings on this is on a par with calling the House of Commons irresponsible on those occasions when great affairs of state are interrupted in order to protect the rights of one individual (as happened, for example, in 1963 over the deportation of Chief Anthony Enahoro to stand trial in Nigeria).

One can point to Dr. Banda of Malawi as an example of an African leader who accepts the realities of his difficult economic position and takes a 'statesmanlike' line – that is, a European line – but it is not a particularly telling argument. For one thing, having lived in a European setting for so many years Dr. Banda has imbibed many of the attitudes of Europe. For another, and this is far more important, it is clear that Dr. Banda is completely out of step with his fellow African leaders and his pan-African standing, if not his political position, is in peril.

There is among adherents to the 'Commonwealth should be British' view a great deal of inconsistency. They deplore in young countries in Africa the development of the one-party state, feeling a natural sense of shock at major departures from the Westminster pattern of democracy. Yet these same people will argue on Southern Rhodesia that it is a pity that the African nationalists have not been united, implying, presumably, that the reflection of differences in the existence of more than one party is a weakness. (It is, and I agree that it is a pity the Southern Rhodesian nationalists have not been united, but one cannot logically hold that view *and* deplore the departure from Westminster democracy.) The whole concept of the Westminster pattern is based on inconsistencies, since the system works only where there is a deep-rooted acceptance of the idea of constructive opposition or alternative government. This idea is not deep-rooted in Africa, nor was it nurtured by the British colonial rulers. They, after all, locked their opponents up rather than paid them salaries to oppose. It is this example which the new rulers have frequently followed – with the basic difference that whereas we released the people we had locked up and handed over power to them, the new rulers usually see power as a goal which once attained must be defended, not as a shuttlecock in the game of politics.

The main need in assessing and evaluating the modern Commonwealth is to accept it for what it is, not for what the romantics would like it to be. Since the Commonwealth is not politically united—and could not be—one of the most obvious ways of accepting it for what it is is in diplomacy. The 'old' Commonwealth was a close-knit family in which the members really did maintain 'English' standards and really did, literally and metaphorically, play cricket. The Commonwealth Relations Office has clung idealistically to the fiction that in the new Commonwealth the rules of cricket are the same. It is an absolutely pointless pretence, but worse than that, it is the reason why in general (and one can always find exceptions) the diplomacy practised by the C.R.O. has never been diplomacy as the Foreign Office knows it. It has been rather the practice of a maternal relationship, the proud and tolerant kindness of the mother country towards her adolescent brood. Anyone travelling round Africa as I did could be sure that in a Foreign Office post he would find able diplomatists who knew what was going on, who were appraising events objectively and expertly, whose feelings of friendliness towards the countries to which they were accredited did not obscure their professionalism. In a C.R.O. post he might find the same kind of people, but too often he would meet dedicated idealists for whom there was something faintly indecent about the business of diplomacy and for whom the work of a High Commission should be not full objective appraisal so much as a vague effusion of good will.

At the beginning of 1965 the Commonwealth and Foreign Services were united in the new Diplomatic Service. Since then, there has been a deliberate policy of posting F.O. men to Commonwealth countries and C.R.O. men to foreign ones to speed the process of fusion. It must be hoped that it is the Foreign Office which proves to be the leaven and the Commonwealth service the lump.

The argument against 'C.R.O. diplomacy' is not only that it does not produce the kind of assessments which the British Government need. It is not even popular with the leaders of the new Commonwealth countries. I remember a conversation with a close friend in a senior position in one of the African High Commissions in London in which he said that he and his colleagues liked the people they dealt with at the C.R.O., but resented their insistence on giving well-meaning advice. They found it much easier to deal with other ministries. More recently, when I was preparing this book, I discussed the whole question of British diplomacy with the head of one of the new Commonwealth states. Without any prompting from me, he said he and his ministers (particularly his ministers) wished Britain were represented in their country by a real professional, even a cold professional, rather than by a man whose attitude was still 'colonial': 'I know all about your difficulties. I know you're inexperienced. Don't worry, I'll sort things out for you.'

It is only fair to add that in my own travels and in London I have always enjoyed excellent relations with British representatives. As my journalistic work was concerned more with Commonwealth than with non-Commonwealth countries I had far more to do with the C.R.O. than with the Foreign Office and many of the officials were not only sincere but extremely shrewd and able. There is none whom I would wish to criticize. I do strongly criticize the whole philosophy of the C.R.O. It was summed up most graphically for me when I was discussing with a C.R.O. official the appointment of Mr. Malcolm Macdonald, then Governor-General of Kenya, to be British High Commissioner there. I questioned whether his naturally close relationship with Mr. Kenyatta's Government, with which as Governor and then Governor-General, he had been on excellent terms, might prejudice his value as a representative of British interests in the eyes of British subjects living in Kenya. Mr. Macdonald's performance of his new role as it happened proved my doubts to be absolutely unfounded, but of course at the time when I put my question no one could know that. The reply was that the policy of the C.R.O. was not to represent British interests so much as to keep on good terms with the local government.

Does the Commonwealth have any meaning? Provided one remembers all the reservations and limitations, I think the answer is that it does.

The very fact that at fairly frequent intervals more than twenty men with countries to run find it worth while to travel to London or elsewhere for discussions with each other–and discussions, incidentally, which never produce and are never intended to produce, policy resolutions–suggests that they do not think the association meaningless.

In some intangible ways the fact of a common heritage helps. To take one example, I have always felt more quickly at home in, say, Nigeria or Ghana, than in any of the French-speaking territories of Africa. This is not because the people in French-speaking Africa are less friendly or less hospitable–the food in restaurants is much more interesting–but because the method of doing things and the way of thought among educated people much more closely resemble our own in the territories which were British. As I explained in an earlier chapter, one of the difficulties about forging a relationship between Senegal and The Gambia has been the fact that the British system of administration and the French do not easily produce mutual understanding.

There are other, more serious, examples than personal impressions. One of the most obvious is the existence of a common military system. It was not particularly difficult, for example, for Canadian army officers to take over training posts in the Ghana Military Academy, as a military mission, when the British officers of the Ghana army were dismissed. The system of command which they were used to was already familiar to the Ghanaians. The value of 'speaking the same language' in this way is most clearly apparent when units from different countries have to co-operate, as they did in the Congo. This is not the place for any comment on the United Nations military operation there, but one thing on which all the experts who have discussed it agree is that the force, necessarily made up of a heterogeneous collection of units from a number of countries, lacked cohesion. The various units came from very different backgrounds. They were trained in widely different methods. Communication between them was difficult, and at times almost non-existent. This problem did not arise between the various Commonwealth armies which were represented. This is not to say, of course, that the Indians, the Nigerians and the Ghanaians always saw eye to eye, or that their respective governments always took exactly the same line. They did not; but at a purely military level there was no danger of misunderstanding.

I had a personal experience of this in 1961 when I visited Albertville, in North Katanga, which was then in a state of some confusion and largely in the hands of anti-Tshombe forces (this was still the era of Katanga's secessionist régime). I was entertained by the Indian Army Medical Corps, the Indian Army being the

N

main U.N. force in the area. Their hospitality was exactly what one would have expected in a British mess–even down to the cup of sweet tea with which I was wakened in the morning.

I have dwelt on these intangible realities of the common Commonwealth heritage because I think they provide the clue to the real meaning of the association. This lies in the common language. I do not mean simply in the fact that in all the Commonwealth countries English is the lingua franca and in most the official language. That, after all, is true of other, non-Commonwealth, countries. The metaphorical common language is far more important, and it is something which can be nurtured. The two great advantages which Commonwealth countries have in their dealings with other Commonwealth countries are first, that in providing technical aid to each other–that is, skilled people–they do not have to cross a thought barrier. The English economist in Zambia, the Nigerian magistrate in Malawi, the Canadian army officer in Ghana can all without difficulty put themselves across. The second advantage is that the educational system in the Commonwealth countries is broadly speaking an 'English' system (there are variants and experiments of course) and this means that the metaphorical common language should continue to flourish.

This does not mean that Commonwealth citizens can, or should, be taught to think alike. Above all it does not mean that Britain– the mother country, the former colonial power, and therefore always under suspicion at least until the ghost of colonialism is completely exorcised–should try to use education as a means of gaining influence. It would be immoral to try, and in any case it would be unlikely to succeed, since the aim of education is to cause people to think for themselves. It does mean that leaders in Commonwealth countries can enjoy the same ways of thought– and may therefore continue to find it worth while to meet each other at intervals to talk, with understanding, about their differences.

Chapter 14

Conflict of Races

In recent years there have been several issues which have shaken the foundations of the Commonwealth, issues which went far deeper than gentlemanly disagreement. One was the question of racism as exemplified in South Africa's apartheid policy. South Africa's policies have certainly not improved, indeed they have become more repressive and more fanatical as the years have gone by, but as far as the Commonwealth was concerned the issue was solved by South Africa's withdrawal. The opportunity arose when South Africa, after deciding to become a republic, had therefore to make a formal application for continued membership of the Commonwealth in her new constitutional status. Towards the end of the Commonwealth Prime Ministers' meeting in 1961, at which South Africa's racial policies were the main topic of discussion, and came under the most strenuous and widespread attack, Dr. Verwoerd decided not to make the application. If he had not thus voluntarily drawn South Africa out of the Commonwealth, there is little doubt that her expulsion would have been demanded by a majority.

Another fundamental issue was the British Government's application for membership of the European Economic Community. In negotiating for entry, the Government undertook to protect Commonwealth interests, and not surprisingly was subjected to a barrage of special pleading from the various Commonwealth members all anxious not to lose the economic benefits of Commonwealth preferences. As is well known, Britain's application for membership was vetoed by President de Gaulle, but not before a great deal of damage had been done to the Commonwealth relationship.

I ought to make it plain that I am personally not in favour of Britain's membership of the E.E.C. (for reasons which have nothing to do with the subject of this book). At the same time, I do not share the views of the romantic 'Commonwealth before

Europe' movement, since its exponents implicitly assert the existence of the Commonwealth as a politico-economic entity which could be seen as an alternative to Europe, and this is against all the facts. There is no doubt at all, for example, that Britain is historically as well as geographically closer to France than to Sabah, or even Sierra Leone. Nor does there seem to be any good reason why Britain, as a Commonwealth member, should not enter another association. The Commonwealth, after all, already encompasses non-aligned nations and members of N.A.T.O. No one has suggested that the African members should not belong to the Organization of African Unity, or that the Caribbean members should not wish to belong to the Organization of American States. It is natural for any government to take an active interest in the affairs of its own region, and the British Government's application to join the European Common Market could be justly interpreted in that light.

The damage to the Commonwealth relationship, in my view, arose from two causes. The first was that the undertaking to protect Commonwealth economic interests was too strong and too specific. It was in effect a promise not to go into Europe if as a result Commonwealth interests would be adversely affected, and some adverse effect was inevitable. It would have been more sensible to say, 'We are going in if we can. We shall do all in our power to protect your interests.'

The second cause, not entirely unconnected with the first, was that the British Government never fully grasped–or at least never fully acknowledged–the essentially political nature of E.E.C. membership. It is true that the negotiations on the economic side were of great complexity and that in mastering them the British negotiating team, and especially Mr. Edward Heath, shewed remarkable skill. Contrary to the impression that was often given however, joining the E.E.C. was not primarily a question of tariffs on wheat or kangaroo tails. It was a question of political power. Because they were so absorbed in the economic matters, the British Government never fully appreciated that for other Commonwealth members, and above all for the young African members, the Common Market issue was first and foremost political.

In September 1962 the Commonwealth Prime Ministers again met in London to discuss, as the most important item on their agenda, Britain's application to the Common Market. For the African members, the E.E.C. was a suspect political grouping and associate membership, which the former French colonies and the former Belgian Congo enjoyed (with substantial economic advantage) was tainted as 'neo-colonialism'. President Nkrumah was the most voluble exponent of this view but it was not by any means his alone. Nigeria, for example, usually regarded in Britain as moderate—which is, incidentally, a meaningless and misleading description of any African government—was quite firmly committed to rejecting associate status handed out as a gift from Whitehall. (Nigeria has subsequently been negotiating on her own with the Common Market, but that is a very different matter, and carries no overtones of continuing dependence on the former colonial power.) Nigeria's opposition was carefully thought out, and soundly based. It was made in the full recognition that rejection of associate status would be costly, and it was made because acceptance would have been even more costly politically.

Nigeria's attitude was an embarrassment for the British Government, and as I found when reporting the Prime Ministers' meeting, they attempted to cover their embarrassment by suggesting that Nigeria's decision was only propaganda and was not really a firm decision at all. This attempt to mislead (which was made by the Foreign Office rather than the Commonwealth Relations Office) did not succeed in blinding journalists and other observers to the facts. It did succeed in exacerbating relations with Nigeria. On one evening, for example, when the Foreign Office line had been peddled assiduously round Fleet Street, I decided to speak to the then Nigerian information attaché—an able and efficient journalist who was as it happens probably the best African press attaché to have served in London. I asked him whether I should believe rumours that were current to the effect that Nigeria was preparing to change its mind over associate status. He immediately replied that he knew where those rumours came from, and added that he would get a comment from his Prime Minister. When it came half an hour later the Prime Minister's comment not only demolished the rumour, but indicated clearly that this ham-fisted British attempt to play Nigerian politics was deeply resented. The attempt would not have been made had Whitehall—or rather the ministers most closely concerned with the Common Market negotiations—possessed a deeper understanding of African feelings.

It is not fair to lay all the blame on Mr. Heath. Mr. Sandys was also concerned with the Common Market talks, and as Commonwealth Secretary was obviously well informed on African policies and attitudes. Nevertheless, Mr. Heath's performance in quite another context – the leadership of the Conservative party through the controversies over Southern Rhodesia's rebellion towards the end of 1965 – confirms the impression that he made at the time of the 1962 Prime Ministers' meeting, namely that he has only a limited understanding of and interest in African affairs.

Southern Rhodesia has been the most recent issue to shake the Commonwealth, and it raises the same spectre as did South Africa in 1961 – racism. It is even more important for the Commonwealth, because Britain, as the focal point of the Commonwealth, is legally responsible for Southern Rhodesia, and has always insisted that this responsibility should be recognized by others. The Rhodesian rebellion, therefore, brought up acutely the question whether the multi-racial nature of the Commonwealth – one of the most constantly reiterated merits that it possesses – is more than a form of words, whether, in short, members, and particularly Britain, are ready to judge a situation impartially on the facts, or will always support those of their own race and colour.

At the time of writing the Southern Rhodesian affair is still developing and any comment on it would certainly be out of date by the time of publication. The issue of racism, however, is of the most fundamental importance, and is worth examining in more detail. It is fundamental not simply to the Commonwealth but to relations between the old nations and the new generally, and to Britain's relations with the new states of Africa and Asia, in or outside the Commonwealth, in particular.

It is a subject on which many people feel deeply. Nothing is to be gained from a pretence that racial prejudice does not exist. It most certainly does, and it is not confined to the ignorant or the stupid, though the more intelligent and educated are at least usually ready to examine it intellectually and not simply to react emotionally. Nor is it confined to one race. It is worth noting, however, that very few, if any, young African governments have expelled white people on racial grounds, though the pressure to adopt racist policies is bound to be strong in a country only recently freed of the 'colonialist yoke'. There have, of course, been expulsions of people who happened to be white, and sometimes they have been

carried out with scant regard for normal standards of consideration and decent behaviour. The reasons for the expulsions, however, some good, some bad, have not been the colour of the skin.
Indeed, in many of the black-ruled states of Africa white people
have been living happily since independence. In several of them
(Zambia and Malawi for example) white men sit in Parliament and
provide leaders of the opposition. In Kenya and Tanzania tolerance has even been carried to the point of having in each country
a white man in the cabinet.

There are things to criticize about all the newly independent
countries and their governments, and in my view the criticisms
should be made without hesitation. They have achieved adult
status, and they should be treated as adults. But to accuse the
young African governments of racism is simply unjustifiable on
the facts. The people in Britain and elsewhere who are ready to
defend white minority rule in South Africa or Southern Rhodesia
with the argument that only by retaining it will white people be
able to continue to live in Africa and civilized standards be maintained, are guilty of tendentiousness (to put it no more strongly)
and furthermore must have a peculiarly twisted view of civilized
standards.

There is a type of enthusiastic 'liberal' who will see nothing bad
about a black government, and who will find reasons why President
Nkrumah should be excused for allowing a political opponent to
die in jail where he had been confined without trial, or who will
argue Dr. Banda's case for calling for the public hanging of a man
before he has even been tried. Such people are wrong. These things
cannot be defended.

Breaches of civilized behaviour are no more defensible, however, when they are made by white men than when they are made
by black. The Government of Dr. Verwoerd in South Africa is
guilty of some of the most blatant persecution ever to have been
carried on in the name of 'civilized standards'. It is not without
significance that a number of the present leaders of South Africa
were supporters of Hitler during the Second World War. And
what are we to think of a Southern Rhodesian régime which
restricts a former prime minister, locks up a leading barrister without trial and without charging him, and introduces legislation
which, among other things, enables people to be detained at the
behest of a particular minister, and with appeal only to that same

minister? Again, it is not without significance that one of the actions of the illegal Smith régime in the first weeks of its seized 'independence' was to try to prevent Rhodesians from listening to the B.B.C. and other outside broadcasting organizations – a move which Hitler made in Germany during the war, presumably for the same reason, a fear of the truth.

One constantly hears the argument that we should support our own kith and kin. At first sight it is a reasonable idea, but anyone who is willing to examine its implications and not simply repeat it parrot-fashion will see that it is tenable only in a situation of racial conflict and then only if you accept the thesis that colour is more important than truth – or to put it epigrammatically, that being white is more important than being right. Even the most dedicated reactionary in the House of Lords would be unlikely to argue that a white man who broke the law in Bournemouth should go unpunished because he was white. If the law-breaker happened to have a fine war record, he would still be punished, and the comment would be 'What a terrible thing that a man with such a fine background should have gone wrong.' Let the same noble lord examine Central Africa, however, and his attitude is quite different. Sometimes – not always – there will be a token criticism of repressive legislation, but the conclusion is that however wrong the white government may have been, what they stand for must be preserved at all costs. The clinching argument is often that they stood by us during the war, and fought in the armed services. It is conveniently forgotten that so did many more black men. Also ignored is the fact that not all the white ex-servicemen believe in illegal action. On December 1, 1965, for example, *The Times* carried a letter from a Rhodesian citizen, an anglican priest, who had been living in Southern Rhodesia since 1960. Before going to Rhodesia he had been rector of my home parish. During the war, he won the M.C. while serving in the British army. He wrote that the only motive for the demand by Mr. Smith and his supporters for independence now, at any price, was to entrench white supremacy in order 'to maintain our present standards'. He doubted whether those standards should be maintained, consisting as they did of plenty of cheap labour and high wages and incomes for Europeans, and he added 'The present illegal régime in this country is based on selfishness and racialism.'

At an early stage in the Rhodesian rebellion, the B.B.C.

CONFLICT OF RACES 197

interviewed a number of ordinary British citizens to ask their view
on what had happened. As is usual in these interviews, many of them
had not the faintest idea what they were talking about, and in these
circumstances the remark 'Well, I support Smith; he's white,
isn't he?' was simply pathetic. When a similar remark is made by
a responsible member of either House of Parliament, it ceases to
be pathetic. It becomes despicable and unprincipled.

In the first of his Reith lectures, 1965, Mr. Robert Gardiner,
who is a Ghanaian and a most able international civil servant, discussed racism, and examined its many facets cogently and calmly.
Early in his talk he said:

> The name was first given to a racial doctrine which began at the end
> of the nineteenth century. According to it, a man's worth was deter-
> mined by the race to which he belonged. In due course the notions
> which make up this doctrine served as the basis of Nazism: a good
> enough reason for making an examination of racism the starting point
> for a study of the problems of a world of peoples.

In pointing out the similarities between the doctrine of Aryan
purity and the belief in the white man's innate superiority, Mr.
Gardiner performed a useful service. If the advocates of 'kith and
kinship' attitudes could be persuaded to think their beliefs through
to their logical conclusion, they would see that they must lead to
an assertion that one group of people should enjoy a privileged
status above other human beings by virtue of race alone. They
might then recognize that their beliefs and Hitler's are not far
apart.

The Southern Rhodesian rebellion brought to the surface in
Britain the latent racism of a large number of people. Faced with
the choice between supporting legality and backing illegal action
done by people of the same race and colour as ourselves, many
British citizens chose the second course. That they did so is a
shaming fact. Even more shaming is the fact that many of the
nation's political leaders went along with the crowd instead of
giving a firm and unequivocal lead on a matter of the highest
principle. This is a criticism which must be levelled at the Conservative Party by any objective observer, whatever his own
political beliefs. For weeks as the Rhodesia crisis developed from
the original illegal declaration of independence Mr. Heath and his
colleagues, though giving broad support to the Government's

measures, quibbled about their details. To examine and evaluate government actions is of course one of the functions of the Opposition, but in doing it, the Conservative front bench avoided making any clear and unambiguous condemnation of the increasing examples of persecution, intolerance and sheer nazism indulged in by the Smith régime. It is true that Mr. Heath stated in Parliament that the whole House abhorred the aspects of the police state introduced in Rhodesia. He did so in a long exchange with the Prime Minister in which he was questioning the wisdom of certain Government measures. He did not think it necessary to repudiate the voluble supporters of the Smith régime within his party, whose utterances received far more publicity than the official party line.

The implications for Britain's domestic politics of party attitudes to the Rhodesia crisis are not my concern here. The implications for Britain's future relations with a large part of the world's population, however, are grave. It is not surprising that Africans and Asians ask whether the multi-racial Commonwealth has any meaning. It is not surprising that the pressures for an all-out race war in southern Africa get steadily stronger. It is difficult to persuade an intelligent African politician that Britain is really prepared to treat him on equal terms as a human being, with faults and merits like any other human being, in face of fanatical outbursts by white extremists, and embarrassed silence by those who disagree with them. How much harder will it be to persuade an unintelligent African of our good faith, when our own actions provide such excellent propaganda material for our enemies?

Rhodesia provoked the most dramatic manifestation of racial intolerance but it was not the first straw in the wind for those who were looking for signs of a genuine adherence to the multi-racial principle. Britain's good name had already suffered badly from the immigration policies of both Conservative and Labour Governments.

The Conservatives introduced the Commonwealth Immigrants Bill at about the time when they were preparing to seek membership of the E.E.C. The timing was unfortunate, since it emphasized an apparent move away from Commonwealth principles. Until this time, it had always been British policy that any Commonwealth citizen should have the absolute right to come to this country. This was in many ways inconvenient for Britain, an overcrowded island, but the principle behind it–the reality of Commonwealth citizenship–was of immense value. Economically, too, the right was of benefit to those Commonwealth countries, notably the West Indies, where years of British neglect had produced economies unable to support decently the whole local population. Mr. Butler, as he then was, introducing the second reading of the Bill as Home Secretary in November 1961, said he did so after 'long and anxious consideration and a considerable reluctance'. Mr. Nigel Fisher, the Conservative M.P. who to his great credit opposed the Bill, and who consistently refused in this and other matters to allow his principles to be outweighed by considerations of political expediency, declared his opposition to 'the whole underlying idea of this Bill'. He drew attention to the 'colour' content of the measure which would certainly affect most strongly coloured Commonwealth immigrants, and he spoke of its cutting the 'rather slender ties' still binding the Commonwealth. In the third reading debate, he said: 'the image of Britain, and, I am sorry to say, of the Conservative Party, has suffered immense harm in the eyes of the coloured nations of the Commonwealth and certainly of the West Indies'.

The Labour Party, then in opposition and led by the late Hugh Gaitskell, strongly condemned the Bill. Gaitskell himself spoke of the debate as being 'a very sad day for the Commonwealth'. Mr. Denis Healey (who became Minister of Defence in the 1964 Labour Government) said: 'We all know that the reason why this Bill has been introduced by the Government at this time is that there are in some parts of these islands big concentrations of coloured people and, as a result, considerable social strains.'

The press, too, emphasized the racial character of the Bill. *The Times* attacked it on several occasions during its progress through the House, and in a leader on February 27, 1962 declared: 'The Bill strikes at the roots of Britain's traditional liberal attitude towards immigration, at the preservation of good Commonwealth relations, and at the belief that Britain is without original sin in the matter of colour discriminatory.' The Bill, *The Times* said, was racially discriminatory in the sense that, though its application was expressly ordered to be on a non-racial basis, the support for it arose out of racial prejudices, pressures and jealousies, and its effects would be greatest on the coloured people of the Commonwealth. *The Guardian* declared it bad in principle. The Archbishop

200   UNSCRAMBLING AN EMPIRE

of Canterbury described it as 'a lamentable and deplorable measure'. The Bill became law.

One might have expected that when they came to power at last in 1964, the Labour Party would have done their best to liberalize the Immigrants Act, if not to repeal it altogether. (Repeal would have been electorally difficult, with their small majority, and in an atmosphere of racial intolerance exemplified by the defeat of Mr. Patrick Gordon Walker by the electors of Smethwick.) What they did, in practice, after being in power for less than a year, was to produce a White Paper *Immigration from the Commonwealth* (Cmnd 2739) proposing the most stringent restrictions on the number of Commonwealth immigrants to be allowed into the country. The White Paper also contained proposals for improving the integration into British life of immigrants. It was nevertheless an infamous document, demonstrating a complete and cynical betrayal of principle by the Labour Party—'a stain upon the reputation of the Labour movement', to quote Mr. Michael Foot in Parliament. *The Times* criticized it strongly but constructively, and suggested among other things that M.P.s should share in the task of educating public opinion out of prejudice against immigrants. By the end of October 1965, the Government were preparing to tone down the measures they had proposed.

The detail of immigration laws is not the point at issue. The significance of the attitude of both Britain's major political parties to immigration by coloured people is that it is yet another indication that the multi-racial equality which they all preach so eloquently is not a matter of principle, but a woolly idea to be hurriedly discarded if it seems likely to be electorally inconvenient. Of course an influx of immigrants poses serious problems for Britain. Of course the development of ghettoes of coloured people can have serious social repercussions. Of course it is difficult to find solutions to these problems. If an important principle is at stake, however, difficulties should be faced rather than the principle sacrificed; and if Britain's official belief in racial equality and in the multi-racial Commonwealth is genuine, then there is no doubt that a principle is involved, and no amount of casuistic explanations and interpretations can alter that fact.

I mentioned in an earlier chapter the criticisms by Dr. Eric Williams of Britain's proprietary attitude to the Commonwealth. In the same talk in July 1965 Dr. Williams made two other significant criticisms. He reminded his listeners that in British Guiana, against the advice of Trinidad and Tobago, the British Government had taken action to alter the constitution in such a way that the colony's government was changed. If it was possible in British Guiana, he asked, why is it not in Southern Rhodesia 'unless it is because one is a government of whites, the other of non-whites'. His second point was that immigration laws, with Europeans getting preference over Commonwealth citizens, would break up the Commonwealth.

Possibly Dr. Williams was overstating his case. Certainly one British answer to his question about Southern Rhodesia is that, having no troops in Southern Rhodesia, the British Government has been in no position to coerce the local government, which has. But that is only half an answer. It would be more convincing to the non-white critics of British policy and attitudes if they could balance it against demonstrable British acceptance of the equality of human beings of whatever colour.

Do the majority of British people accept this ideal of equal status? Do our political leaders accept it? They may, but until they are prepared to maintain their belief more loudly and more persistently than those who proclaim the paramount importance of 'kith and kinship', the possibility of racial conflict in Africa and elsewhere grows steadily greater and more terrifying.

Chapter 15

Looking Ahead

IN the old days of empire the aims of policy were clear. When once the decision had been made to transform empire into Commonwealth, the aims were different, but still the policy-makers could work to a purpose. Unlike the Portuguese, whose colonial mission was, and is, assimilation, the creation of black Portuguese in territories which are formally not colonies but overseas provinces of Portugal, the British have for many years accepted that colonial territories were held in trust. They must be led towards independence. Colonial dependence must be only a temporary phase.

For years this has not been a matter of political controversy. There has been no conflict between the British parties on the principles which should guide colonial policy, however strongly the methods have been argued. The big change in recent years has been in the speed at which power has been devolved. The 'wind of change', much quoted phrase, signified not a change of direction but an acceleration of tempo. Inevitably, the acceleration aroused opposition among the more cautious as well as among the outright reactionaries, and to that extent colonial policy, in the last few years of colonialism, has been more controversial than before. Even so, the controversies have not been fundamental.

It is against this background of general acceptance of broad aims that my criticisms have been made. The strategy of decolonization, it seems to me, has been sound as well as acceptable. It is the tactics that have tended to go awry.

To a great extent, the errors that have been made can be attributed to lack of preparation and lack of thought, both in turn due to lack of time as the pace of change quickened and steady evolution became a mad and headlong rush. It is perhaps not surprising that some of the constitutional tasks have been imperfectly finished, as I have attempted to shew. It is not surprising that there have been inconsistencies such as the different approach to West Africa on the one hand and East and Central Africa on the other, or even the different approach to the white settler countries and the others within a particular area. It has rarely been possible, in the past few years, for the British Government to find a solution to one colonial problem before another, or several others, have urgently demanded solutions in turn. At various times two or three major constitutional exercises have been carried on simultaneously and ministers and senior officials have been forced to perform a kind of constitutional quick change act to satisfy several sets of importunate colonial politicians at once.

Tribute is due to the hard work and devotion of these ministers and officials. The fact remains that they have had too many things on their plate at once and have therefore often been concerned more with finding ways to be properly and decently rid of colonial encumbrances than with seeking viable long-term new relationships. Solutions have been evolved which looked all right on paper, but already there have been enough examples of the failure of paper solutions to shew that they are really no complete answer. Lancaster House conferences have their place in the scheme of things. Arguments about the franchise, or about minority safeguards or bills of rights, are necessary. They are valuable, however, only in so far as they reflect realities, just as domestic laws are respected only when they reflect the general will. What purpose, after all, was served by the long and tedious arguments over Kenya's complicated regional constitution? What possibilities of peaceful advancement have been secured by the 1961 constitution of Southern Rhodesia? In both cases the answer is none, or almost none. In Kenya the constitution was virtually meaningless because it did not have the support of the people who were going to run the country. In Southern Rhodesia, the constitution failed because one group of people – the African nationalists – ignored it, and those who used it were able to make mincemeat of its ostensible limitations on local power, even before the unilateral declaration of independence.

Too often the Whitehall aim has been simply to produce tidy packages which would be acceptable in Westminster or in the United Nations, with little recognition that the packages were to be used by people. At its worst, this attitude was cynicism but far more frequently it has been a lack of understanding arising, as I have suggested, from overwork and lack of time to think. An inevitable result of this surfeit of immediate problems to be dealt with by the same small group of people, has been the neglect of matters which did not cry out so urgently for attention. The best example of this, as I have explained earlier, is the fact that no coherent policy has been worked out for the smaller territories. It is a serious omission because finding a reasonable solution for countries which cannot simply stand on their own feet is bound to be difficult and in an age when independence has come to be considered an inalienable human right, it will be very difficult indeed.

One of the most obvious mistakes was the decision to abolish the separate post of Colonial Secretary. In time, of course, the successful pursuit of colonial policy must mean the abolition of both Colonial Secretary and Colonial Office (though some department or sub-department will have to take responsibility for the remaining dependencies). When the amalgamation of the two offices was made in the summer of 1962, however, each post still offered quite a sufficient challenge for one able man. Already by that time the Colonial Office suffered from the brevity of Mr. Maudling's incumbency. He hardly had time to get fully to grips with the many tasks before him before he was moved on to the Treasury. It would have been far better if Mr. Macleod had been permitted to stay and finish the job he was doing and doing well. When, on Mr. Maudling's translation, the Colonial Office became in effect an adjunct of the Commonwealth Relations Office, Britain's colonial mission received a most serious setback. For one thing morale at the Colonial Office fell. It was true that the office remained a separate entity, but the Secretary of State conducted business from Downing Street, not Great Smith Street, and it needed more than usual dedication on the part of the Colonial Office civil servants to believe that they were now working in anything but a backwater. For another thing, Mr. Sandys, for all his excellent qualities—which include courage and an exceptional capacity for hard work—was by no means ideally suited to the job. He was not popular among African leaders, who saw him as the advocate of the hated Federation. His toughness and tenacity in negotiation were valuable assets for dealing with awkward people, but they needed to be combined with a greater understanding and sympathy for the aspirations of colonial peoples than he appeared to possess. His willingness to work long hours, often well into the night, was unfortunately combined with an unwillingness to delegate even routine tasks of drafting to officials. With international crises demanding his attention in his role as Commonwealth

Secretary he did not have the time—no man could have had time—to give full thought to colonial problems. He certainly had no time to do much long-term thinking. In any case, the qualities required of a good Colonial Secretary are not at all the same as those required of a good Commonwealth Relations Secretary. Their functions are totally different. Their approach needs to be totally different, too. To expect any one man to wear the two hats at once is to ask him to embody a dichotomy. Not surprisingly, it did not work. The difficulties were apparent, in a slightly different form, when two Secretaries of State were responsible for different aspects of colonial policy in central Africa.

The Labour Party were surely wise to separate the two posts again when they came to office in 1964. (One immediate result, incidentally, was a marked rise in morale in the office.) The last stages of dismantling an empire are at least as complex as the earlier ones, and until the job is finished it is right for it to be entrusted to a senior minister, and for the Colonial Office officials to know that their work is still taken seriously.

Essentially, however, what is left for the Colonial Office is a clearing up operation. Far more important now is to build new relationships between ourselves and the former colonies. As I hope I have demonstrated, this is no routine task. Trust and understanding do not grow automatically on either side. Without being a complete pessimist, one cannot be sanguine in face of the many causes of mistrust and misunderstanding which could so easily destroy the efforts of years of honourable colonial involvement. Southern Rhodesia is more than a difficult legal puzzle. It is a rock on which relations between the new nations and the old, the black and the white, could founder. The same is true of the southern African territories of Basutoland, Bechuanaland and Swaziland. If the British Government leaves them as hostages, to sink or swim at the will of South Africa, Britain's long record of independence freely given will be tarnished. In what may broadly be called colonial policy, the problems that remain are those of race and geography. To solve them, we need quickly to regain a sense of mission and purpose. If we cannot do so, if we fail to ensure that the standards we proclaim have real meaning, that independent countries can be truly independent, that equality means equality for all, then the new international relationship which we have tried to create in dismantling an empire will be founded on quicksand.

o

Index